The Equalizer - A Musical Method

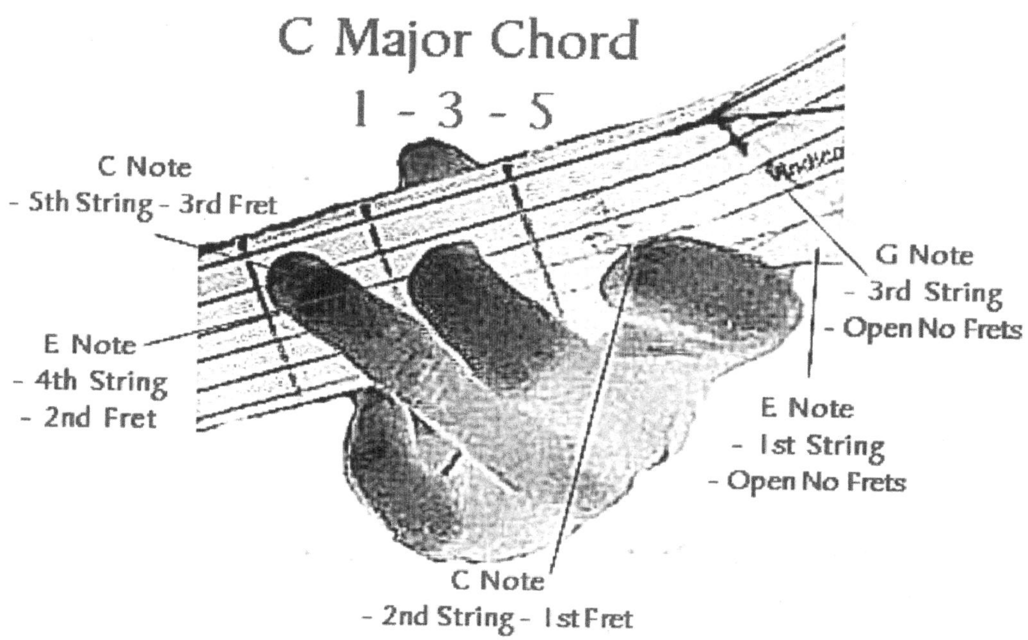

Key of C M3

C	C#	D	D#	E	F	F#	G	G#	A	A#	B	C	C#	D	D#	E	F	F#	G	G#	A	A#	B	C
12	11	10	9	8	7	6	5	4	3	2	1	0	1	2	3	4	5	6	7	8	9	10	11	12
M3	P4		P5		M6		M7	OC		M2		M3	P4		P5		M6		M7	OC		M2		M3
		D5		m6		m7			m2		m3			D5		m6		m7			m2		m3	

BY CRAIG BLAKE

The Equalizer
- A Musical Method

Dedication

This book is dedicated to the loving memory of my father Allan Blake who was a dear friend and supported my every venture.

Preface

Craig Blake's method is a must-have for the practicing and professional musician. **The Equalizer - A Musical Method** is a natural and gravitational approach to song-writing by means of numbers and a balance-beam. Simply, create chord progressions with the balance-beam charts, then apply the compatible scales/scale-sets.

I have developed and written The Equalizer - A Musical Method with my own philosophy in mind: Realizing the potential of your instrument, is the instrument to realizing your potential.

The Equalizer - A Musical Method can be incorporated by novice, intermediate, and advanced musicians, and it can also be applied to any genre of music such as rock, blues, jazz, country etc., by incorporating the balance beam - it opened up a-whole-new-world of possibilities. My mission: Strive to design a system for music-writing that would ultimately assist the composer during the development process.

TABLE OF CONTENTS

Introduction to The Equalizer
- A Musical Method

The Equalizer - A Musical Method is a revolutionary system for composing music by means of numbers and a balance-beam. It virtually eliminates all guesswork during chord and note selection.

Basic Music Theory to Assist in the Understanding of the Mechanics of 'The Equalizer'. There are twelve notes used in music, and they repeat. The twelve notes are adopted from the letters of the alphabet A, B, C, D, E, F and G respectively. In addition, there are sharps (#) symbolized by a number sign, they are notes that are one note, or a semitone above the natural note (no sharps or flats).
Note: There is no sharp between B and C and there is no sharp between E and F. The series of twelve notes are as follows: A, A#, B, C, C#, D, D#, E, F ,F#, G, and G#. The given series of notes are also known as an octave. This is why the twelfth fret - frets are the metal bars that runs parallel across the neck or fingerboard - is marked with two dots, on the guitar.

In standard tuning, when you strike the open (no frets) A string, it vibrates at a frequency of 440 hertz. In other words, it vibrates 440 times per second. However, if you strike the twelfth fret on the same string, which is also an A note, it vibrates exactly twice as high in pitch - a frequency of 880 times per second. This is because the twelfth fret is one octave higher than the open A note - no frets. This is demonstrated in figure 1.

Figure 1

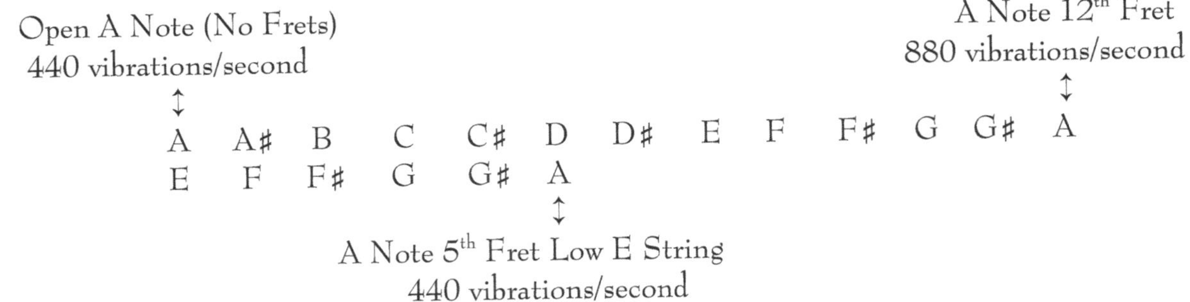

Tuning the Guitar

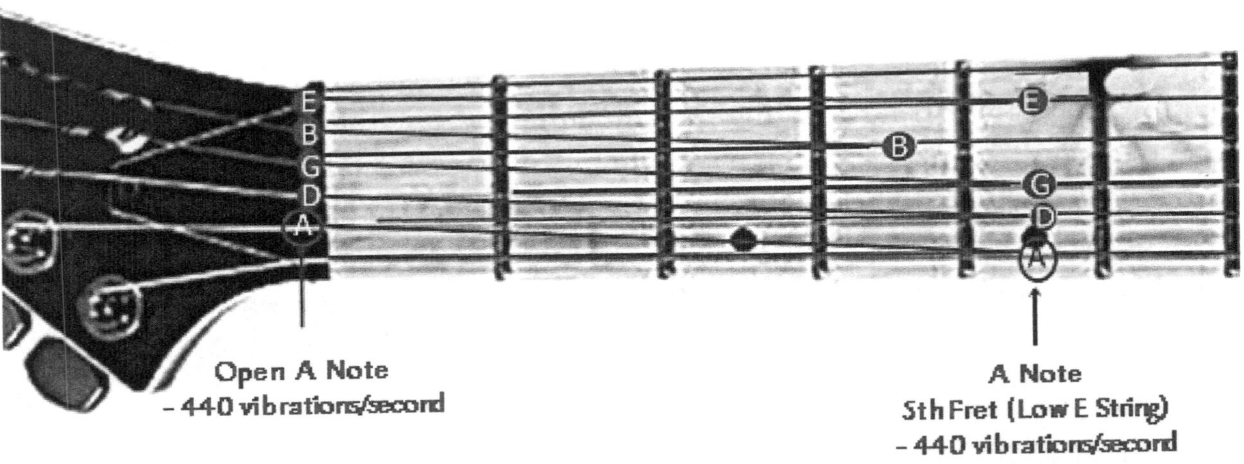

Figure 2 demonstrates all of the names of the open strings on the guitar.

Figure 2

High E (Thinnest) ➪ E
Open B
Open G
Open D
Open A
Low E (Thickest) ➪ E

Figure 3 demonstrates all of the E notes over the entire fret-board, as shown on a twenty- four-fret guitar. Numbers indicate E notes and their respective octaves.

Figure 3

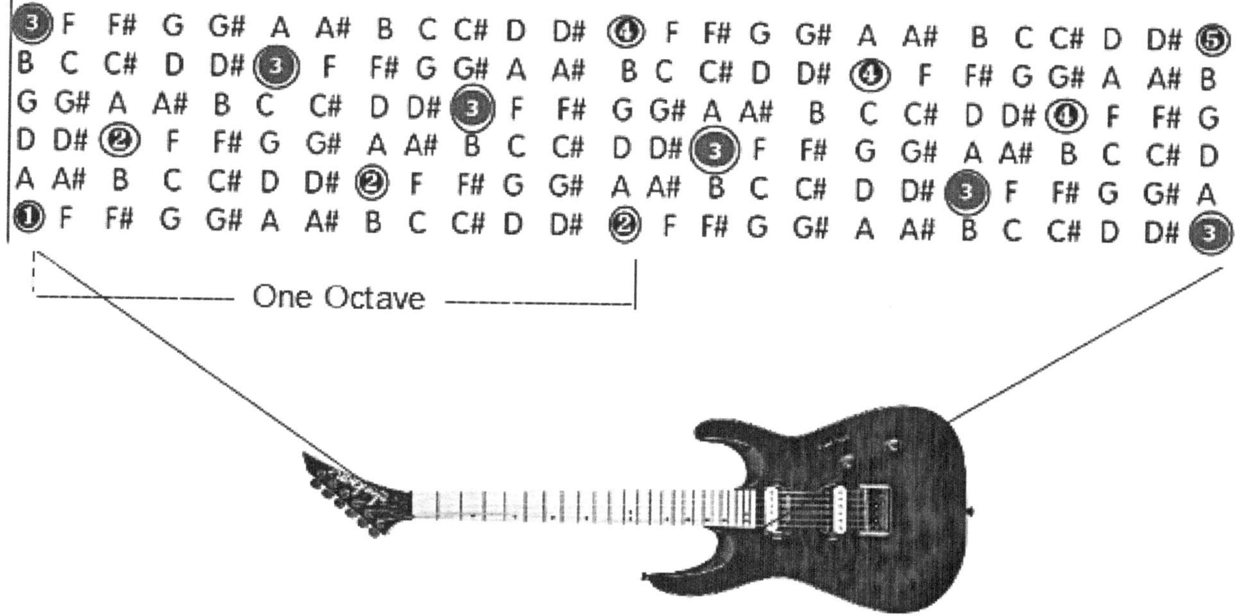

The Mechanics of The Equalizer

The Equalizer can be applied by both the novice and advanced musician, allowing you to analyze the note or chord relations, as well as isolate the pitches for rhythm and phrasing purposes, by means of numbers and a balance beam - this alone is a superlative benefit.

The key note (root) - the main note that chords are derived from, and songs are played around- is always represented by zero (0). This is the balance point of the key note on the balance beam. Your objective is to total the numbers which represent the notes on one side of the beam with the numbers on the opposite side of the beam - spanning two octaves. For example, let's look at the key of "E" as demonstrated in figure 4.

In standard rock or country music, the three basic chords are: E (key or root), A and B. First, you start with E represented by zero on the balance beam, move to the left side of the beam, and you'll find that the A is positioned directly above the number seven (7). Now, to balance the beam, while using three (3) notes - for a three note chord progression, you have to move to the seventh (7th) position on the right side of the beam, which in this case is B. So now, in the key of "E" you have E, A, and B respectfully. You may employ as many, or any combination of notes that you like - as long as they're balanced on the beam.

Figure 4

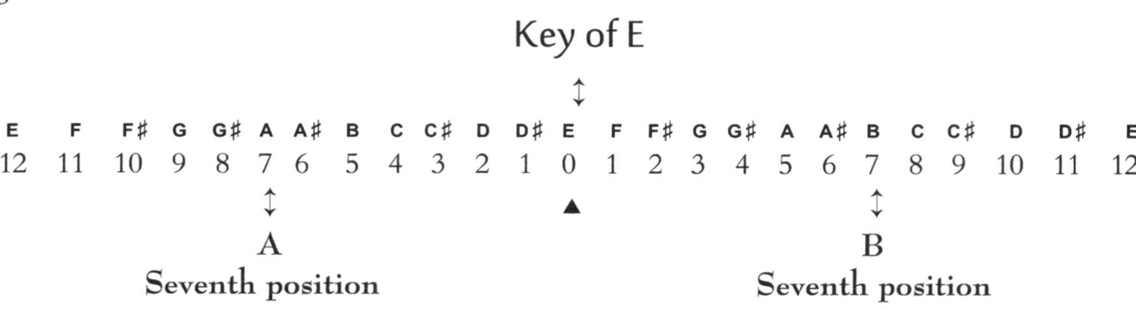

With The Equalizer - A Musical Method, the possibilities are virtually unlimited, for exploring and expressing your creativity as a musician. You can also apply more technical techniques. For example, there are twelve given notes in an octave which mean there are twelve different intervals or degrees - the difference in sound between two notes - which determine the chord names. Major chords are written as capital M, and minor chords are written as lowercase m.

The twelve different interval names are:
E-F= minor second, E-F#= Major second, E-G= minor third, E-G#= Major third, E-A= Perfect fourth, E-A# = Diminished fifth, E-B= Perfect fifth, E-C= minor sixth, E-C#= Major sixth, E-D= minor seventh, E-D#= Major seventh, and E-E= Octave. As shown in figure 5.

Figure 5

The low E string (guitar) - Thickest

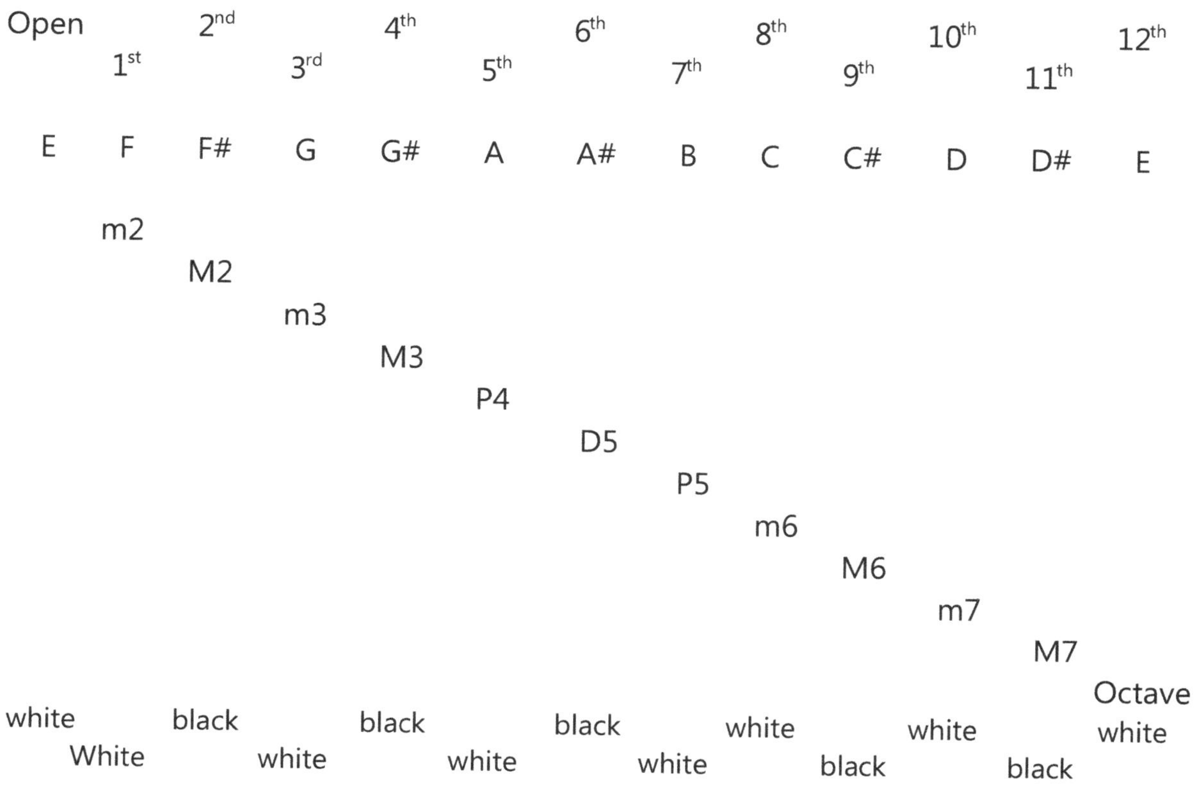

The notes of the piano - the white keys represent natural (Diatonic) notes: A, B, C, D etc. The black keys represent sharps/flats - depending on which way they are applied.

The twelve intervals shown in their respective positions on the balance beam - Key of C. As shown in figure 6.

Figure 6

Key of C Octave (OC)

C	C♯	D	D♯	E	F	F♯	G	G♯	A	A♯	B	C	C♯	D	D♯	E	F	F♯	G	G♯	A	A♯	B	C
12	11	10	9	8	7	6	5	4	3	2	1	0	1	2	3	4	5	6	7	8	9	10	11	12
OC		M2		M3	P4		P5		M6		M7	OC		M2		M3	P4		P5		M6		M7	OC
	m2		m3			D5		m6		m7			m2		m3			D5		m6		m7		

The Major Scale

The major scale is the direct result of starting with C and extracting all of the sharps, so you're left with the seven natural tones C, D, E, F, G, A, and B. The major scale is the father of all scales, and consists of seven tones. All other scales are derived from or alterations of the Major scale.

A A# B **C** C# **D** D# **E** **F** F# **G** G# **A** A# **B** **C** C# D D# E

C Major Scale

C	D	E	F	G	A	B	C
1	2	3	4	5	6	7	1

The Major Scale is a seven tone scale. It consists of seven modes. There are three Major modes, three minor modes, and one diminished mode within the major scale. The first mode of the major scale is Ionian C-C.

Modes can be thought of as a scale within a scale. Thus, a five tone scale will have five modes, and a seven tone scale will have seven modes etc.

Mode 1	**Ionian**	- Major -	C		D		E	F		G		A		B C
Mode 2	**Dorian**	- Minor -	D		E	F		G		A		B	C		D
Mode 3	**Phrygian**	- Minor -	E	F		G		A		B	C		D		E
Mode 4	**Lydian**	- Major -	F		G		A		B	C		D		E	F
Mode 5	**Mixolydian**	- Major -	G		A		B	C		D		E	F		G
Mode 6	**Aeolian**	- Minor -	A		B	C		D		E	F		G		A
Mode 7	**Locrian**	- Diminished -	B	C		D		E	F		G		A		B

Scales and Scale-Sets.

Scales are a selected series of notes extracted from the twelve tones of the octave. There are five, six, seven, eight, and nine tone scales. The twelve tone scale is also know as the chromatic scale.

Scale-Sets are the collective groups of five, six, seven, eight, and nine tone compatible scales used for any given interval or chord.

Try taking an interval then playing the first scale in the in the five tone scales for that interval. Then, try playing the first six tone scale out of the six tone scales etc. Also, try mixing or blending scales five tone with seven tone, and five tone with nine tone etc.

Balance-Beam Charts

The Balance-Beam Charts work on the same principle as a balance-scale. They are based on gravity, weight and numbers. The center of the beam - represented by "0" zero - is the key. Notice how the key note - represented by twelve - is balanced at both ends. To balance the beam, add a note or notes on one side of the beam, then add or distribute notes on the opposite side of the beam, when the sum of numbers on both sides are equal, the beam is level or balanced. Therefore, the selected notes, intervals or chords will work together.

It is a generally accepted principle in music that the fifth interval or chord resolves gracefully back home to the key. So, keep the fifth in mind, while balancing the beam for your chord progressions.

The twelve intervals shown in their respective positions on the balance beam - Key of C. As shown in figure 6.

Figure 6

Key of C Octave (OC)

C	C♯	D	D♯	E	F	F♯	G	G♯	A	A♯	B	C	C♯	D	D♯	E	F	F♯	G	G♯	A	A♯	B	C
12	11	10	9	8	7	6	5	4	3	2	1	0	1	2	3	4	5	6	7	8	9	10	11	12
OC		M2		M3	P4		P5		M6		M7	OC		M2		M3	P4		P5		M6		M7	OC
	m2		m3			D5		m6		m7			m2		m3			D5		m6		m7		

Balance - Beam Chart Components

Key of C M3

C	C♯	D	D♯	E	F	F♯	G	G♯	A	A♯	B	C	C♯	D	D♯	E	F	F♯	G	G♯	A	A♯	B	C
12	11	10	9	8	7	6	5	4	3	2	1	0	1	2	3	4	5	6	7	8	9	10	11	12
M3	P4		P5		M6		M7	OC		M2		M3	P4		P5		M6		M7	OC		M2		M3
		D5		m6		m7			m2		m3			D5		m6		m7			m2		m3	

Notes

There are twelve notes spanning two octaves on the balance-beam for a total of twenty four notes.

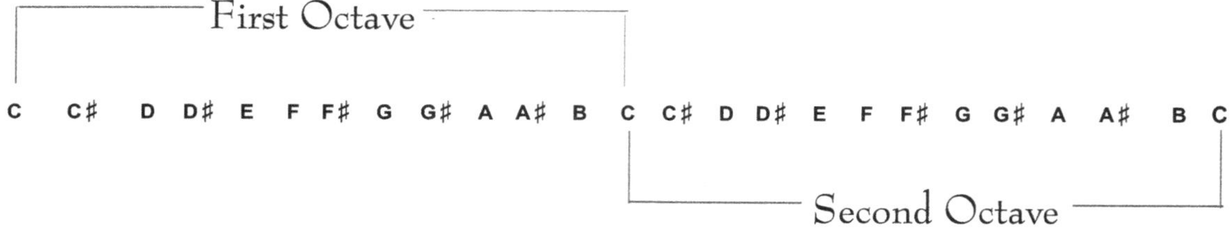

Numbers

The numbers start at the center of the beam and runs in opposing directions. Zero (0) center, always represents the key. The numbers represent the weight and respective positions of the intervals.

12 11 10 9 8 7 6 5 4 3 2 1 0 1 2 3 4 5 6 7 8 9 10 11 12

Intervals

Intervals are the building blocks of chords. Strike one string, and you produce a note. Strike two strings, and you are playing an interval. Strike three or more strings, and you are producing a chord.

M3 P4 D5 P5 m6 M6 m7 M7 OC m2 M2 m3 M3 P4 D5 P5 m6 M6 m7 M7 OC m2 M2 m3 M3

Keys

Key of A

A	A♯	B	C	C♯	D	D♯	E	F	F♯	G	G♯	A	A♯	B	C	C♯	D	D♯	E	F	F♯	G	G♯	A
12	11	10	9	8	7	6	5	4	3	2	1	0	1	2	3	4	5	6	7	8	9	10	11	12

Key of A♯

A♯	B	C	C♯	D	D♯	E	F	F♯	G	G♯	A	A♯	B	C	C♯	D	D♯	E	F	F♯	G	G♯	A	A♯
12	11	10	9	8	7	6	5	4	3	2	1	0	1	2	3	4	5	6	7	8	9	10	11	12

Key of B

B	C	C♯	D	D♯	E	F	F♯	G	G♯	A	A♯	B	C	C♯	D	D♯	E	F	F♯	G	G♯	A	A♯	B
12	11	10	9	8	7	6	5	4	3	2	1	0	1	2	3	4	5	6	7	8	9	10	11	12

Key of C

C	C♯	D	D♯	E	F	F♯	G	G♯	A	A♯	B	C	C♯	D	D♯	E	F	F♯	G	G♯	A	A♯	B	C
12	11	10	9	8	7	6	5	4	3	2	1	0	1	2	3	4	5	6	7	8	9	10	11	12

Key of C♯

C♯	D	D♯	E	F	F♯	G	G♯	A	A♯	B	C	C♯	D	D♯	E	F	F♯	G	G♯	A	A♯	B	C	C♯
12	11	10	9	8	7	6	5	4	3	2	1	0	1	2	3	4	5	6	7	8	9	10	11	12

Key of D

D	D♯	E	F	F♯	G	G♯	A	A♯	B	C	C♯	D	D♯	E	F	F♯	G	G♯	A	A♯	B	C	C♯	D
12	11	10	9	8	7	6	5	4	3	2	1	0	1	2	3	4	5	6	7	8	9	10	11	12

Key of D♯

D♯	E	F	F♯	G	G♯	A	A♯	B	C	C♯	D	D♯	E	F	F♯	G	G♯	A	A♯	B	C	C♯	D	D♯
12	11	10	9	8	7	6	5	4	3	2	1	0	1	2	3	4	5	6	7	8	9	10	11	12

Key of E

E	F	F♯	G	G♯	A	A♯	B	C	C♯	D	D♯	E	F	F♯	G	G♯	A	A♯	B	C	C♯	D	D♯	E
12	11	10	9	8	7	6	5	4	3	2	1	0	1	2	3	4	5	6	7	8	9	10	11	12

Key of F

F	F♯	G	G♯	A	A♯	B	C	C♯	D	D♯	E	F	F♯	G	G♯	A	A♯	B	C	C♯	D	D♯	E	F
12	11	10	9	8	7	6	5	4	3	2	1	0	1	2	3	4	5	6	7	8	9	10	11	12

Key of F♯

F♯	G	G♯	A	A♯	B	C	C♯	D	D♯	E	F	F♯	G	G♯	A	A♯	B	C	C♯	D	D♯	E	F	F♯
12	11	10	9	8	7	6	5	4	3	2	1	0	1	2	3	4	5	6	7	8	9	10	11	12

Key of G

G	G♯	A	A♯	B	C	C♯	D	D♯	E	F	F♯	G	G♯	A	A♯	B	C	C♯	D	D♯	E	F	F♯	G
12	11	10	9	8	7	6	5	4	3	2	1	0	1	2	3	4	5	6	7	8	9	10	11	12

Key of G♯

G♯	A	A♯	B	C	C♯	D	D♯	E	F	F♯	G	G♯	A	A♯	B	C	C♯	D	D♯	E	F	F♯	G	G♯
12	11	10	9	8	7	6	5	4	3	2	1	0	1	2	3	4	5	6	7	8	9	10	11	12

Balance-Beam Charts

Keys and Intervals

Key of A (OC)

A	A♯	B	C	C♯	D	D♯	E	F	F♯	G	G♯	A	A♯	B	C	C♯	D	D♯	E	F	F♯	G	G♯	A
12	11	10	9	8	7	6	5	4	3	2	1	0	1	2	3	4	5	6	7	8	9	10	11	12
OC		M2		M3	P4		P5		M6		M7	OC		M2		M3	P4		P5		M6		M7	OC
	m2		m3			D5		m6		m7			m2		m3			D5		m6		m7		

Key of A m2

A	A♯	B	C	C♯	D	D♯	E	F	F♯	G	G♯	A	A♯	B	C	C♯	D	D♯	E	F	F♯	G	G♯	A
12	11	10	9	8	7	6	5	4	3	2	1	0	1	2	3	4	5	6	7	8	9	10	11	12
	M2		M3	P4		P5		M6		M7	OC		M2		M3	P4		P5		M6		M7	OC	
m2		m3			D5		m6		m7			m2		m3			D5		m6		m7			m2

Key of A M2

A	A♯	B	C	C♯	D	D♯	E	F	F♯	G	G♯	A	A♯	B	C	C♯	D	D♯	E	F	F♯	G	G♯	A
12	11	10	9	8	7	6	5	4	3	2	1	0	1	2	3	4	5	6	7	8	9	10	11	12
M2		M3	P4		P5		M6		M7	OC		M2		M3	P4		P5		M6		M7	OC		M2
	m3			D5		m6		m7			m2		m3			D5		m6		m7			m2	

Key of A m3

A	A♯	B	C	C♯	D	D♯	E	F	F♯	G	G♯	A	A♯	B	C	C♯	D	D♯	E	F	F♯	G	G♯	A
12	11	10	9	8	7	6	5	4	3	2	1	0	1	2	3	4	5	6	7	8	9	10	11	12
	M3	P4		P5		M6		M7	OC		M2		M3	P4		P5		M6		M7	OC		M2	
m3			D5		m6		m7			m2		m3			D5		m6		m7			m2		m3

Key of A M3

A	A♯	B	C	C♯	D	D♯	E	F	F♯	G	G♯	A	A♯	B	C	C♯	D	D♯	E	F	F♯	G	G♯	A
12	11	10	9	8	7	6	5	4	3	2	1	0	1	2	3	4	5	6	7	8	9	10	11	12
M3	P4		P5		M6		M7	OC		M2		M3	P4		P5		M6		M7	OC		M2		M3
		D5		m6		m7			m2		m3			D5		m6		m7			m2		m3	

Key of A P4

A	A♯	B	C	C♯	D	D♯	E	F	F♯	G	G♯	A	A♯	B	C	C♯	D	D♯	E	F	F♯	G	G♯	A
12	11	10	9	8	7	6	5	4	3	2	1	0	1	2	3	4	5	6	7	8	9	10	11	12
P4		P5		M6		M7	OC		M2		M3	P4		P5		M6		M7	OC		M2		M3	P4
	D5		m6		m7			m2		m3			D5		m6		m7			m2		m3		

Key of A D5

A	A♯	B	C	C♯	D	D♯	E	F	F♯	G	G♯	A	A♯	B	C	C♯	D	D♯	E	F	F♯	G	G♯	A
12	11	10	9	8	7	6	5	4	3	2	1	0	1	2	3	4	5	6	7	8	9	10	11	12
	P5		M6		M7	OC		M2		M3	P4		P5		M6		M7	OC		M2		M3	P4	
D5		m6		m7			m2		m3			D5		m6		m7			m2		m3			D5

Key of A P5

A	A♯	B	C	C♯	D	D♯	E	F	F♯	G	G♯	A	A♯	B	C	C♯	D	D♯	E	F	F♯	G	G♯	A
12	11	10	9	8	7	6	5	4	3	2	1	0	1	2	3	4	5	6	7	8	9	10	11	12
P5		M6		M7	OC		M2		M3	P4		P5		M6		M7	OC		M2		M3	P4		P5
	m6		m7			m2		m3			D5		m6		m7			m2		m3			D5	

Key of A m6

A	A♯	B	C	C♯	D	D♯	E	F	F♯	G	G♯	A	A♯	B	C	C♯	D	D♯	E	F	F♯	G	G♯	A
12	11	10	9	8	7	6	5	4	3	2	1	0	1	2	3	4	5	6	7	8	9	10	11	12
	M6		M7	OC		M2		M3	P4		P5		M6		M7	OC		M2		M3	P4		P5	
m6		m7			m2		m3			D5		m6		m7			m2		m3			D5		m6

Key of A M6

A	A♯	B	C	C♯	D	D♯	E	F	F♯	G	G♯	A	A♯	B	C	C♯	D	D♯	E	F	F♯	G	G♯	A
12	11	10	9	8	7	6	5	4	3	2	1	0	1	2	3	4	5	6	7	8	9	10	11	12
M6		M7	OC		M2		M3	P4		P5		M6		M7	OC		M2		M3	P4		P5		M6
	m7			m2		m3			D5		m6		m7			m2		m3			D5		m6	

Key of A m7

A	A♯	B	C	C♯	D	D♯	E	F	F♯	G	G♯	A	A♯	B	C	C♯	D	D♯	E	F	F♯	G	G♯	A
12	11	10	9	8	7	6	5	4	3	2	1	0	1	2	3	4	5	6	7	8	9	10	11	12
	M7	OC		M2		M3	P4		P5		M6		M7	OC		M2		M3	P4		P5		M6	
m7			m2		m3			D5		m6		m7			m2		m3			D5		m6		m7

Key of A M7

A	A♯	B	C	C♯	D	D♯	E	F	F♯	G	G♯	A	A♯	B	C	C♯	D	D♯	E	F	F♯	G	G♯	A
12	11	10	9	8	7	6	5	4	3	2	1	0	1	2	3	4	5	6	7	8	9	10	11	12
M7	OC		M2		M3	P4		P5		M6		M7	OC		M2		M3	P4		P5		M6		M7
		m2		m3			D5		m6		m7			m2		m3			D5		m6		m7	

Key of A♯ (OC)

A♯	B	C	C♯	D	D♯	E	F	F♯	G	G♯	A	A♯	B	C	C♯	D	D♯	E	F	F♯	G	G♯	A	A♯
12	11	10	9	8	7	6	5	4	3	2	1	0	1	2	3	4	5	6	7	8	9	10	11	12
OC		M2		M3	P4		P5		M6		M7	OC		M2		M3	P4		P5		M6		M7	OC
	m2		m3			D5		m6		m7			m2		m3			D5		m6		m7		

Key of A♯ m2

A♯	B	C	C♯	D	D♯	E	F	F♯	G	G♯	A	A♯	B	C	C♯	D	D♯	E	F	F♯	G	G♯	A	A♯
12	11	10	9	8	7	6	5	4	3	2	1	0	1	2	3	4	5	6	7	8	9	10	11	12
	M2		M3	P4		P5		M6		M7	OC		M2		M3	P4		P5		M6		M7	OC	
m2		m3			D5		m6		m7			m2		m3			D5		m6		m7			m2

Key of A♯ M2

A♯	B	C	C♯	D	D♯	E	F	F♯	G	G♯	A	A♯	B	C	C♯	D	D♯	E	F	F♯	G	G♯	A	A♯
12	11	10	9	8	7	6	5	4	3	2	1	0	1	2	3	4	5	6	7	8	9	10	11	12
M2		M3	P4		P5		M6		M7	OC		M2		M3	P4		P5		M6		M7	OC		M2
	m3			D5		m6		m7			m2		m3			D5		m6		m7			m2	

Key of A♯ m3

A♯	B	C	C♯	D	D♯	E	F	F♯	G	G♯	A	A♯	B	C	C♯	D	D♯	E	F	F♯	G	G♯	A	A♯
12	11	10	9	8	7	6	5	4	3	2	1	0	1	2	3	4	5	6	7	8	9	10	11	12
	M3	P4		P5		M6		M7	OC		M2		M3	P4		P5		M6		M7	OC		M2	
m3			D5		m6		m7			m2		m3			D5		m6		m7			m2		m3

Key of A♯ M3

A♯	B	C	C♯	D	D♯	E	F	F♯	G	G♯	A	A♯	B	C	C♯	D	D♯	E	F	F♯	G	G♯	A	A♯
12	11	10	9	8	7	6	5	4	3	2	1	0	1	2	3	4	5	6	7	8	9	10	11	12
M3	P4		P5		M6		M7	OC		M2		M3	P4		P5		M6		M7	OC		M2		M3
		D5		m6		m7			m2		m3			D5		m6		m7			m2		m3	

Key of A♯ P4

A♯	B	C	C♯	D	D♯	E	F	F♯	G	G♯	A	A♯	B	C	C♯	D	D♯	E	F	F♯	G	G♯	A	A♯
12	11	10	9	8	7	6	5	4	3	2	1	0	1	2	3	4	5	6	7	8	9	10	11	12
P4		P5		M6		M7	OC		M2		M3	P4		P5		M6		M7	OC		M2		M3	P4
	D5		m6		m7			m2		m3			D5		m6		m7			m2		m3		

Key of A♯ D5

A♯	B	C	C♯	D	D♯	E	F	F♯	G	G♯	A	A♯	B	C	C♯	D	D♯	E	F	F♯	G	G♯	A	A♯
12	11	10	9	8	7	6	5	4	3	2	1	0	1	2	3	4	5	6	7	8	9	10	11	12
	P5		M6		M7	OC		M2		M3	P4		P5		M6		M7	OC		M2		M3	P4	
D5		m6		m7			m2		m3			D5		m6		m7			m2		m3			D5

Key of A♯ P5

A♯	B	C	C♯	D	D♯	E	F	F♯	G	G♯	A	A♯	B	C	C♯	D	D♯	E	F	F♯	G	G♯	A	A♯
12	11	10	9	8	7	6	5	4	3	2	1	0	1	2	3	4	5	6	7	8	9	10	11	12
P5		M6		M7	OC		M2		M3	P4		P5		M6		M7	OC		M2		M3	P4		P5
	m6		m7			m2		m3			D5		m6		m7			m2		m3			D5	

Key of A♯ m6

A♯	B	C	C♯	D	D♯	E	F	F♯	G	G♯	A	A♯	B	C	C♯	D	D♯	E	F	F♯	G	G♯	A	A♯
12	11	10	9	8	7	6	5	4	3	2	1	0	1	2	3	4	5	6	7	8	9	10	11	12
	M6		M7	OC		M2		M3	P4		P5		M6		M7	OC		M2		M3	P4		P5	
m6		m7			m2		m3			D5		m6		m7			m2		m3			D5		m6

Key of A♯ M6

A♯	B	C	C♯	D	D♯	E	F	F♯	G	G♯	A	A♯	B	C	C♯	D	D♯	E	F	F♯	G	G♯	A	A♯
12	11	10	9	8	7	6	5	4	3	2	1	0	1	2	3	4	5	6	7	8	9	10	11	12
M6		M7	OC		M2		M3	P4		P5		M6		M7	OC		M2		M3	P4		P5		M6
	m7			m2		m3			D5		m6		m7			m2		m3			D5		m6	

Key of A♯ m7

A♯	B	C	C♯	D	D♯	E	F	F♯	G	G♯	A	A♯	B	C	C♯	D	D♯	E	F	F♯	G	G♯	A	A♯
12	11	10	9	8	7	6	5	4	3	2	1	0	1	2	3	4	5	6	7	8	9	10	11	12
	M7	OC		M2		M3	P4		P5		M6		M7	OC		M2		M3	P4		P5		M6	
m7			m2		m3			D5		m6		m7			m2		m3			D5		m6		m7

Key of A♯ M7

A♯	B	C	C♯	D	D♯	E	F	F♯	G	G♯	A	A♯	B	C	C♯	D	D♯	E	F	F♯	G	G♯	A	A♯
12	11	10	9	8	7	6	5	4	3	2	1	0	1	2	3	4	5	6	7	8	9	10	11	12
M7	OC		M2		M3	P4		P5		M6		M7	OC		M2		M3	P4		P5		M6		M7
		m2		m3			D5		m6		m7			m2		m3			D5		m6		m7	

Key of B (OC)

B	C	C♯	D	D♯	E	F	F♯	G	G♯	A	A♯	B	C	C♯	D	D♯	E	F	F♯	G	G♯	A	A♯	B
12	11	10	9	8	7	6	5	4	3	2	1	0	1	2	3	4	5	6	7	8	9	10	11	12
OC		M2		M3	P4		P5		M6		M7	OC		M2		M3	P4		P5		M6		M7	OC
	m2		m3			D5		m6		m7			m2		m3			D5		m6		m7		

Key of B m2

B	C	C♯	D	D♯	E	F	F♯	G	G♯	A	A♯	B	C	C♯	D	D♯	E	F	F♯	G	G♯	A	A♯	B
12	11	10	9	8	7	6	5	4	3	2	1	0	1	2	3	4	5	6	7	8	9	10	11	12
	M2		M3	P4		P5		M6		M7	OC		M2		M3	P4		P5		M6		M7	OC	
m2		m3			D5		m6		m7			m2		m3			D5		m6		m7			m2

Key of B M2

B	C	C♯	D	D♯	E	F	F♯	G	G♯	A	A♯	B	C	C♯	D	D♯	E	F	F♯	G	G♯	A	A♯	B
12	11	10	9	8	7	6	5	4	3	2	1	0	1	2	3	4	5	6	7	8	9	10	11	12
M2		M3	P4		P5		M6		M7	OC		M2		M3	P4		P5		M6		M7	OC		M2
	m3			D5		m6		m7			m2		m3			D5		m6		m7			m2	

Key of B m3

B	C	C♯	D	D♯	E	F	F♯	G	G♯	A	A♯	B	C	C♯	D	D♯	E	F	F♯	G	G♯	A	A♯	B
12	11	10	9	8	7	6	5	4	3	2	1	0	1	2	3	4	5	6	7	8	9	10	11	12
	M3	P4		P5		M6		M7	OC		M2		M3	P4		P5		M6		M7	OC		M2	
m3			D5		m6		m7			m2		m3			D5		m6		m7			m2		m3

Key of B M3

B	C	C♯	D	D♯	E	F	F♯	G	G♯	A	A♯	B	C	C♯	D	D♯	E	F	F♯	G	G♯	A	A♯	B
12	11	10	9	8	7	6	5	4	3	2	1	0	1	2	3	4	5	6	7	8	9	10	11	12
M3	P4		P5		M6		M7	OC		M2		M3	P4		P5		M6		M7	OC		M2		M3
		D5		m6		m7			m2		m3			D5		m6		m7			m2		m3	

Key of B P4

B	C	C♯	D	D♯	E	F	F♯	G	G♯	A	A♯	B	C	C♯	D	D♯	E	F	F♯	G	G♯	A	A♯	B
12	11	10	9	8	7	6	5	4	3	2	1	0	1	2	3	4	5	6	7	8	9	10	11	12
P4		P5		M6		M7	OC		M2		M3	P4		P5		M6		M7	OC		M2		M3	P4
	D5		m6		m7			m2		m3			D5		m6		m7			m2		m3		

Key of B D5

B	C	C♯	D	D♯	E	F	F♯	G	G♯	A	A♯	B	C	C♯	D	D♯	E	F	F♯	G	G♯	A	A♯	B
12	11	10	9	8	7	6	5	4	3	2	1	0	1	2	3	4	5	6	7	8	9	10	11	12
	P5		M6		M7	OC		M2		M3	P4		P5		M6		M7	OC		M2		M3	P4	
D5		m6		m7			m2		m3			D5		m6		m7			m2		m3			D5

Key of B P5

B	C	C♯	D	D♯	E	F	F♯	G	G♯	A	A♯	B	C	C♯	D	D♯	E	F	F♯	G	G♯	A	A♯	B
12	11	10	9	8	7	6	5	4	3	2	1	0	1	2	3	4	5	6	7	8	9	10	11	12
P5		M6		M7	OC		M2		M3	P4		P5		M6		M7	OC		M2		M3	P4		P5
	m6		m7			m2		m3			D5		m6		m7			m2		m3			D5	

Key of B m6

B	C	C♯	D	D♯	E	F	F♯	G	G♯	A	A♯	B	C	C♯	D	D♯	E	F	F♯	G	G♯	A	A♯	B
12	11	10	9	8	7	6	5	4	3	2	1	0	1	2	3	4	5	6	7	8	9	10	11	12
	M6		M7	OC		M2		M3	P4		P5		M6		M7	OC		M2		M3	P4		P5	
m6		m7			m2		m3			D5		m6		m7			m2		m3			D5		m6

Key of B M6

B	C	C♯	D	D♯	E	F	F♯	G	G♯	A	A♯	B	C	C♯	D	D♯	E	F	F♯	G	G♯	A	A♯	B
12	11	10	9	8	7	6	5	4	3	2	1	0	1	2	3	4	5	6	7	8	9	10	11	12
M6		M7	OC		M2		M3	P4		P5		M6		M7	OC		M2		M3	P4		P5		M6
	m7			m2		m3			D5		m6		m7			m2		m3			D5		m6	

Key of B m7

B	C	C♯	D	D♯	E	F	F♯	G	G♯	A	A♯	B	C	C♯	D	D♯	E	F	F♯	G	G♯	A	A♯	B
12	11	10	9	8	7	6	5	4	3	2	1	0	1	2	3	4	5	6	7	8	9	10	11	12
	M7	OC		M2		M3	P4		P5		M6		M7	OC		M2		M3	P4		P5		M6	
m7			m2		m3			D5		m6		m7			m2		m3			D5		m6		m7

Key of B M7

B	C	C♯	D	D♯	E	F	F♯	G	G♯	A	A♯	B	C	C♯	D	D♯	E	F	F♯	G	G♯	A	A♯	B
12	11	10	9	8	7	6	5	4	3	2	1	0	1	2	3	4	5	6	7	8	9	10	11	12
M7	OC		M2		M3	P4		P5		M6		M7	OC		M2		M3	P4		P5		M6		M7
		m2		m3			D5		m6		m7			m2		m3			D5		m6		m7	

Key of C (OC)

C	C♯	D	D♯	E	F	F♯	G	G♯	A	A♯	B	C	C♯	D	D♯	E	F	F♯	G	G♯	A	A♯	B	C
12	11	10	9	8	7	6	5	4	3	2	1	0	1	2	3	4	5	6	7	8	9	10	11	12
OC		M2		M3	P4		P5		M6		M7	OC		M2		M3	P4		P5		M6		M7	OC
	m2		m3			D5		m6		m7			m2		m3			D5		m6		m7		

Key of C m2

C	C♯	D	D♯	E	F	F♯	G	G♯	A	A♯	B	C	C♯	D	D♯	E	F	F♯	G	G♯	A	A♯	B	C
12	11	10	9	8	7	6	5	4	3	2	1	0	1	2	3	4	5	6	7	8	9	10	11	12
	M2		M3	P4		P5		M6		M7	OC		M2		M3	P4		P5		M6		M7	OC	
m2		m3			D5		m6		m7			m2		m3			D5		m6		m7			m2

Key of C M2

C	C♯	D	D♯	E	F	F♯	G	G♯	A	A♯	B	C	C♯	D	D♯	E	F	F♯	G	G♯	A	A♯	B	C
12	11	10	9	8	7	6	5	4	3	2	1	0	1	2	3	4	5	6	7	8	9	10	11	12
M2		M3	P4		P5		M6		M7	OC		M2		M3	P4		P5		M6		M7	OC		M2
	m3			D5		m6		m7			m2		m3			D5		m6		m7			m2	

Key of C m3

C	C♯	D	D♯	E	F	F♯	G	G♯	A	A♯	B	C	C♯	D	D♯	E	F	F♯	G	G♯	A	A♯	B	C
12	11	10	9	8	7	6	5	4	3	2	1	0	1	2	3	4	5	6	7	8	9	10	11	12
	M3	P4		P5		M6		M7	OC		M2		M3	P4		P5		M6		M7	OC		M2	
m3			D5		m6		m7			m2		m3			D5		m6		m7			m2		m3

Key of C M3

C	C♯	D	D♯	E	F	F♯	G	G♯	A	A♯	B	C	C♯	D	D♯	E	F	F♯	G	G♯	A	A♯	B	C
12	11	10	9	8	7	6	5	4	3	2	1	0	1	2	3	4	5	6	7	8	9	10	11	12
M3	P4		P5		M6		M7	OC		M2		M3	P4		P5		M6		M7	OC		M2		M3
		D5		m6		m7			m2		m3			D5		m6		m7			m2		m3	

Key of C P4

C	C♯	D	D♯	E	F	F♯	G	G♯	A	A♯	B	C	C♯	D	D♯	E	F	F♯	G	G♯	A	A♯	B	C
12	11	10	9	8	7	6	5	4	3	2	1	0	1	2	3	4	5	6	7	8	9	10	11	12
P4		P5		M6		M7	OC		M2		M3	P4		P5		M6		M7	OC		M2		M3	P4
	D5		m6		m7			m2		m3			D5		m6		m7			m2		m3		

Key of C D5

C	C♯	D	D♯	E	F	F♯	G	G♯	A	A♯	B	C	C♯	D	D♯	E	F	F♯	G	G♯	A	A♯	B	C
12	11	10	9	8	7	6	5	4	3	2	1	0	1	2	3	4	5	6	7	8	9	10	11	12
	P5		M6		M7	OC		M2		M3	P4		P5		M6		M7	OC		M2		M3	P4	
D5		m6		m7			m2		m3			D5		m6		m7			m2		m3			D5

Key of C P5

C	C♯	D	D♯	E	F	F♯	G	G♯	A	A♯	B	C	C♯	D	D♯	E	F	F♯	G	G♯	A	A♯	B	C
12	11	10	9	8	7	6	5	4	3	2	1	0	1	2	3	4	5	6	7	8	9	10	11	12
P5		M6		M7	OC		M2		M3	P4		P5		M6		M7	OC		M2		M3	P4		P5
	m6		m7			m2		m3			D5		m6		m7			m2		m3			D5	

Key of C m6

C	C♯	D	D♯	E	F	F♯	G	G♯	A	A♯	B	C	C♯	D	D♯	E	F	F♯	G	G♯	A	A♯	B	C
12	11	10	9	8	7	6	5	4	3	2	1	0	1	2	3	4	5	6	7	8	9	10	11	12
	M6		M7	OC		M2		M3	P4		P5		M6		M7	OC		M2		M3	P4		P5	
m6		m7			m2		m3			D5		m6		m7			m2		m3			D5		m6

Key of C M6

C	C♯	D	D♯	E	F	F♯	G	G♯	A	A♯	B	C	C♯	D	D♯	E	F	F♯	G	G♯	A	A♯	B	C
12	11	10	9	8	7	6	5	4	3	2	1	0	1	2	3	4	5	6	7	8	9	10	11	12
M6		M7	OC		M2		M3	P4		P5		M6		M7	OC		M2		M3	P4		P5		M6
	m7			m2		m3			D5		m6		m7			m2		m3			D5		m6	

Key of C m7

C	C♯	D	D♯	E	F	F♯	G	G♯	A	A♯	B	C	C♯	D	D♯	E	F	F♯	G	G♯	A	A♯	B	C
12	11	10	9	8	7	6	5	4	3	2	1	0	1	2	3	4	5	6	7	8	9	10	11	12
	M7	OC		M2		M3	P4		P5		M6		M7	OC		M2		M3	P4		P5		M6	
m7			m2		m3			D5		m6		m7			m2		m3			D5		m6		m7

Key of C M7

C	C♯	D	D♯	E	F	F♯	G	G♯	A	A♯	B	C	C♯	D	D♯	E	F	F♯	G	G♯	A	A♯	B	C
12	11	10	9	8	7	6	5	4	3	2	1	0	1	2	3	4	5	6	7	8	9	10	11	12
M7	OC		M2		M3	P4		P5		M6		M7	OC		M2		M3	P4		P5		M6		M7
		m2		m3			D5		m6		m7			m2		m3			D5		m6		m7	

Key of C♯ (OC)

C♯	D	D♯	E	F	F♯	G	G♯	A	A♯	B	C	C♯	D	D♯	E	F	F♯	G	G♯	A	A♯	B	C	C♯
12	11	10	9	8	7	6	5	4	3	2	1	0	1	2	3	4	5	6	7	8	9	10	11	12
OC		M2		M3	P4		P5		M6		M7	OC		M2		M3	P4		P5		M6		M7	OC
	m2		m3			D5		m6		m7			m2		m3			D5		m6		m7		

Key of C♯ m2

C♯	D	D♯	E	F	F♯	G	G♯	A	A♯	B	C	C♯	D	D♯	E	F	F♯	G	G♯	A	A♯	B	C	C♯
12	11	10	9	8	7	6	5	4	3	2	1	0	1	2	3	4	5	6	7	8	9	10	11	12
	M2		M3	P4		P5		M6		M7	OC		M2		M3	P4		P5		M6		M7	OC	
m2		m3			D5		m6		m7			m2		m3			D5		m6		m7			m2

Key of C♯ M2

C♯	D	D♯	E	F	F♯	G	G♯	A	A♯	B	C	C♯	D	D♯	E	F	F♯	G	G♯	A	A♯	B	C	C♯
12	11	10	9	8	7	6	5	4	3	2	1	0	1	2	3	4	5	6	7	8	9	10	11	12
M2		M3	P4		P5		M6		M7	OC		M2		M3	P4		P5		M6		M7	OC		M2
	m3			D5		m6		m7			m2		m3			D5		m6		m7			m2	

Key of C♯ m3

C♯	D	D♯	E	F	F♯	G	G♯	A	A♯	B	C	C♯	D	D♯	E	F	F♯	G	G♯	A	A♯	B	C	C♯
12	11	10	9	8	7	6	5	4	3	2	1	0	1	2	3	4	5	6	7	8	9	10	11	12
	M3	P4		P5		M6		M7	OC		M2		M3	P4		P5		M6		M7	OC		M2	
m3			D5		m6		m7			m2		m3			D5		m6		m7			m2		m3

Key of C♯ M3

C♯	D	D♯	E	F	F♯	G	G♯	A	A♯	B	C	C♯	D	D♯	E	F	F♯	G	G♯	A	A♯	B	C	C♯
12	11	10	9	8	7	6	5	4	3	2	1	0	1	2	3	4	5	6	7	8	9	10	11	12
M3	P4		P5		M6		M7	OC		M2		M3	P4		P5		M6		M7	OC		M2		M3
		D5		m6		m7			m2		m3			D5		m6		m7			m2		m3	

Key of C♯ P4

C♯	D	D♯	E	F	F♯	G	G♯	A	A♯	B	C	C♯	D	D♯	E	F	F♯	G	G♯	A	A♯	B	C	C♯
12	11	10	9	8	7	6	5	4	3	2	1	0	1	2	3	4	5	6	7	8	9	10	11	12
P4		P5		M6		M7	OC		M2		M3	P4		P5		M6		M7	OC		M2		M3	P4
	D5		m6		m7			m2		m3			D5		m6		m7			m2		m3		

Key of C♯ D5

C♯	D	D♯	E	F	F♯	G	G♯	A	A♯	B	C	C♯	D	D♯	E	F	F♯	G	G♯	A	A♯	B	C	C♯
12	11	10	9	8	7	6	5	4	3	2	1	0	1	2	3	4	5	6	7	8	9	10	11	12
	P5		M6		M7	OC		M2		M3	P4		P5		M6		M7	OC		M2		M3	P4	
D5		m6		m7			m2		m3			D5		m6		m7			m2		m3			D5

Key of C♯ P5

C♯	D	D♯	E	F	F♯	G	G♯	A	A♯	B	C	C♯	D	D♯	E	F	F♯	G	G♯	A	A♯	B	C	C♯
12	11	10	9	8	7	6	5	4	3	2	1	0	1	2	3	4	5	6	7	8	9	10	11	12
P5		M6		M7	OC		M2		M3	P4		P5		M6		M7	OC		M2		M3	P4		P5
	m6		m7			m2		m3			D5		m6		m7			m2		m3			D5	

Key of C♯ m6

C♯	D	D♯	E	F	F♯	G	G♯	A	A♯	B	C	C♯	D	D♯	E	F	F♯	G	G♯	A	A♯	B	C	C♯
12	11	10	9	8	7	6	5	4	3	2	1	0	1	2	3	4	5	6	7	8	9	10	11	12
	M6		M7	OC		M2		M3	P4		P5		M6		M7	OC		M2		M3	P4		P5	
m6		m7			m2		m3			D5		m6		m7			m2		m3			D5		m6

Key of C♯ M6

C♯	D	D♯	E	F	F♯	G	G♯	A	A♯	B	C	C♯	D	D♯	E	F	F♯	G	G♯	A	A♯	B	C	C♯
12	11	10	9	8	7	6	5	4	3	2	1	0	1	2	3	4	5	6	7	8	9	10	11	12
M6		M7	OC		M2		M3	P4		P5		M6		M7	OC		M2		M3	P4		P5		M6
	m7			m2		m3			D5		m6		m7			m2		m3			D5		m6	

Key of C♯ m7

C♯	D	D♯	E	F	F♯	G	G♯	A	A♯	B	C	C♯	D	D♯	E	F	F♯	G	G♯	A	A♯	B	C	C♯
12	11	10	9	8	7	6	5	4	3	2	1	0	1	2	3	4	5	6	7	8	9	10	11	12
	M7	OC		M2		M3	P4		P5		M6		M7	OC		M2		M3	P4		P5		M6	
m7			m2		m3			D5		m6		m7			m2		m3			D5		m6		m7

Key of C♯ M7

C♯	D	D♯	E	F	F♯	G	G♯	A	A♯	B	C	C♯	D	D♯	E	F	F♯	G	G♯	A	A♯	B	C	C♯
12	11	10	9	8	7	6	5	4	3	2	1	0	1	2	3	4	5	6	7	8	9	10	11	12
M7	OC		M2		M3	P4		P5		M6		M7	OC		M2		M3	P4		P5		M6		M7
		m2		m3			D5		m6		m7			m2		m3			D5		m6		m7	

Key of D (OC)

D	D♯	E	F	F♯	G	G♯	A	A♯	B	C	C♯	D	D♯	E	F	F♯	G	G♯	A	A♯	B	C	C♯	D
12	11	10	9	8	7	6	5	4	3	2	1	0	1	2	3	4	5	6	7	8	9	10	11	12
OC		M2		M3	P4		P5		M6		M7	OC		M2		M3	P4		P5		M6		M7	OC
	m2		m3			D5		m6		m7			m2		m3			D5		m6		m7		

Key of D m2

D	D♯	E	F	F♯	G	G♯	A	A♯	B	C	C♯	D	D♯	E	F	F♯	G	G♯	A	A♯	B	C	C♯	D
12	11	10	9	8	7	6	5	4	3	2	1	0	1	2	3	4	5	6	7	8	9	10	11	12
	M2		M3	P4		P5		M6		M7	OC		M2		M3	P4		P5		M6		M7	OC	
m2		m3			D5		m6		m7			m2		m3			D5		m6		m7			m2

Key of D M2

D	D♯	E	F	F♯	G	G♯	A	A♯	B	C	C♯	D	D♯	E	F	F♯	G	G♯	A	A♯	B	C	C♯	D
12	11	10	9	8	7	6	5	4	3	2	1	0	1	2	3	4	5	6	7	8	9	10	11	12
M2		M3	P4		P5		M6		M7	OC		M2		M3	P4		P5		M6		M7	OC		M2
	m3			D5		m6		m7			m2		m3			D5		m6		m7			m2	

Key of D m3

D	D♯	E	F	F♯	G	G♯	A	A♯	B	C	C♯	D	D♯	E	F	F♯	G	G♯	A	A♯	B	C	C♯	D
12	11	10	9	8	7	6	5	4	3	2	1	0	1	2	3	4	5	6	7	8	9	10	11	12
	M3	P4		P5		M6		M7	OC		M2		M3	P4		P5		M6		M7	OC		M2	
m3			D5		m6		m7			m2		m3			D5		m6		m7			m2		m3

Key of D M3

D	D♯	E	F	F♯	G	G♯	A	A♯	B	C	C♯	D	D♯	E	F	F♯	G	G♯	A	A♯	B	C	C♯	D
12	11	10	9	8	7	6	5	4	3	2	1	0	1	2	3	4	5	6	7	8	9	10	11	12
M3	P4		P5		M6		M7	OC		M2		M3	P4		P5		M6		M7	OC		M2		M3
		D5		m6		m7			m2		m3			D5		m6		m7			m2		m3	

Key of D P4

D	D♯	E	F	F♯	G	G♯	A	A♯	B	C	C♯	D	D♯	E	F	F♯	G	G♯	A	A♯	B	C	C♯	D
12	11	10	9	8	7	6	5	4	3	2	1	0	1	2	3	4	5	6	7	8	9	10	11	12
P4		P5		M6		M7	OC		M2		M3	P4		P5		M6		M7	OC		M2		M3	P4
	D5		m6		m7			m2		m3			D5		m6		m7			m2		m3		

Key of D D5

D	D♯	E	F	F♯	G	G♯	A	A♯	B	C	C♯	D	D♯	E	F	F♯	G	G♯	A	A♯	B	C	C♯	D
12	11	10	9	8	7	6	5	4	3	2	1	0	1	2	3	4	5	6	7	8	9	10	11	12
	P5		M6		M7	OC		M2		M3	P4		P5		M6		M7	OC		M2		M3	P4	
D5		m6		m7			m2		m3			D5		m6		m7			m2		m3			D5

Key of D P5

D	D♯	E	F	F♯	G	G♯	A	A♯	B	C	C♯	D	D♯	E	F	F♯	G	G♯	A	A♯	B	C	C♯	D
12	11	10	9	8	7	6	5	4	3	2	1	0	1	2	3	4	5	6	7	8	9	10	11	12
P5		M6		M7	OC		M2		M3	P4		P5		M6		M7	OC		M2		M3	P4		P5
	m6		m7			m2		m3			D5		m6		m7			m2		m3			D5	

Key of D m6

D	D♯	E	F	F♯	G	G♯	A	A♯	B	C	C♯	D	D♯	E	F	F♯	G	G♯	A	A♯	B	C	C♯	D
12	11	10	9	8	7	6	5	4	3	2	1	0	1	2	3	4	5	6	7	8	9	10	11	12
	M6		M7	OC		M2		M3	P4		P5		M6		M7	OC		M2		M3	P4		P5	
m6		m7			m2		m3			D5		m6		m7			m2		m3			D5		m6

Key of D M6

D	D♯	E	F	F♯	G	G♯	A	A♯	B	C	C♯	D	D♯	E	F	F♯	G	G♯	A	A♯	B	C	C♯	D
12	11	10	9	8	7	6	5	4	3	2	1	0	1	2	3	4	5	6	7	8	9	10	11	12
M6		M7	OC		M2		M3	P4		P5		M6		M7	OC		M2		M3	P4		P5		M6
	m7			m2		m3			D5		m6		m7			m2		m3			D5		m6	

Key of D m7

D	D♯	E	F	F♯	G	G♯	A	A♯	B	C	C♯	D	D♯	E	F	F♯	G	G♯	A	A♯	B	C	C♯	D
12	11	10	9	8	7	6	5	4	3	2	1	0	1	2	3	4	5	6	7	8	9	10	11	12
	M7	OC		M2		M3	P4		P5		M6		M7	OC		M2		M3	P4		P5		M6	
m7			m2		m3			D5		m6		m7			m2		m3			D5		m6		m7

Key of D M7

D	D♯	E	F	F♯	G	G♯	A	A♯	B	C	C♯	D	D♯	E	F	F♯	G	G♯	A	A♯	B	C	C♯	D
12	11	10	9	8	7	6	5	4	3	2	1	0	1	2	3	4	5	6	7	8	9	10	11	12
M7	OC		M2		M3	P4		P5		M6		M7	OC		M2		M3	P4		P5		M6		M7
		m2		m3			D5		m6		m7			m2		m3			D5		m6		m7	

Key of D♯ (OC)

D♯	E	F	F♯	G	G♯	A	A♯	B	C	C♯	D	D♯	E	F	F♯	G	G♯	A	A♯	B	C	C♯	D	D♯
12	11	10	9	8	7	6	5	4	3	2	1	0	1	2	3	4	5	6	7	8	9	10	11	12
OC		M2		M3	P4		P5		M6		M7	OC		M2		M3	P4		P5		M6		M7	OC
	m2		m3			D5		m6		m7			m2		m3			D5		m6		m7		

Key of D♯ m2

D♯	E	F	F♯	G	G♯	A	A♯	B	C	C♯	D	D♯	E	F	F♯	G	G♯	A	A♯	B	C	C♯	D	D♯
12	11	10	9	8	7	6	5	4	3	2	1	0	1	2	3	4	5	6	7	8	9	10	11	12
	M2		M3	P4		P5		M6		M7	OC		M2		M3	P4		P5		M6		M7	OC	
m2		m3			D5		m6		m7			m2		m3			D5		m6		m7			m2

Key of D♯ M2

D♯	E	F	F♯	G	G♯	A	A♯	B	C	C♯	D	D♯	E	F	F♯	G	G♯	A	A♯	B	C	C♯	D	D♯
12	11	10	9	8	7	6	5	4	3	2	1	0	1	2	3	4	5	6	7	8	9	10	11	12
M2		M3	P4		P5		M6		M7	OC		M2		M3	P4		P5		M6		M7	OC		M2
	m3			D5		m6		m7			m2		m3			D5		m6		m7			m2	

Key of D♯ m3

D♯	E	F	F♯	G	G♯	A	A♯	B	C	C♯	D	D♯	E	F	F♯	G	G♯	A	A♯	B	C	C♯	D	D♯
12	11	10	9	8	7	6	5	4	3	2	1	0	1	2	3	4	5	6	7	8	9	10	11	12
	M3	P4		P5		M6		M7	OC		M2		M3	P4		P5		M6		M7	OC		M2	
m3			D5		m6		m7			m2		m3			D5		m6		m7			m2		m3

Key of D♯ M3

D♯	E	F	F♯	G	G♯	A	A♯	B	C	C♯	D	D♯	E	F	F♯	G	G♯	A	A♯	B	C	C♯	D	D♯
12	**11**	**10**	**9**	**8**	**7**	**6**	**5**	**4**	**3**	**2**	**1**	**0**	**1**	**2**	**3**	**4**	**5**	**6**	**7**	**8**	**9**	**10**	**11**	**12**
M3	P4	D5	P5	m6	M6	m7	M7	OC	m2	M2	m3	M3	P4	D5	P5	m6	M6	m7	M7	OC	m2	M2	m3	M3

Key of D♯ P4

D♯	E	F	F♯	G	G♯	A	A♯	B	C	C♯	D	D♯	E	F	F♯	G	G♯	A	A♯	B	C	C♯	D	D♯
12	**11**	**10**	**9**	**8**	**7**	**6**	**5**	**4**	**3**	**2**	**1**	**0**	**1**	**2**	**3**	**4**	**5**	**6**	**7**	**8**	**9**	**10**	**11**	**12**
P4	D5	P5	m6	M6	m7	M7	OC	m2	M2	m3	M3	P4	D5	P5	m6	M6	m7	M7	OC	m2	M2	m3	M3	P4

Key of D♯ D5

D♯	E	F	F♯	G	G♯	A	A♯	B	C	C♯	D	D♯	E	F	F♯	G	G♯	A	A♯	B	C	C♯	D	D♯
12	**11**	**10**	**9**	**8**	**7**	**6**	**5**	**4**	**3**	**2**	**1**	**0**	**1**	**2**	**3**	**4**	**5**	**6**	**7**	**8**	**9**	**10**	**11**	**12**
D5	P5	m6	M6	m7	M7	OC	m2	M2	m3	M3	P4	D5	P5	m6	M6	m7	M7	OC	m2	M2	m3	M3	P4	D5

Key of D♯ P5

D♯	E	F	F♯	G	G♯	A	A♯	B	C	C♯	D	D♯	E	F	F♯	G	G♯	A	A♯	B	C	C♯	D	D♯
12	**11**	**10**	**9**	**8**	**7**	**6**	**5**	**4**	**3**	**2**	**1**	**0**	**1**	**2**	**3**	**4**	**5**	**6**	**7**	**8**	**9**	**10**	**11**	**12**
P5	m6	M6	m7	M7	OC	m2	M2	m3	M3	P4	D5	P5	m6	M6	m7	M7	OC	m2	M2	m3	M3	P4	D5	P5

Key of D♯ m6

D♯	E	F	F♯	G	G♯	A	A♯	B	C	C♯	D	D♯	E	F	F♯	G	G♯	A	A♯	B	C	C♯	D	D♯
12	**11**	**10**	**9**	**8**	**7**	**6**	**5**	**4**	**3**	**2**	**1**	**0**	**1**	**2**	**3**	**4**	**5**	**6**	**7**	**8**	**9**	**10**	**11**	**12**
m6	M6	m7	M7	OC	m2	M2	m3	M3	P4	D5	P5	m6	M6	m7	M7	OC	m2	M2	m3	M3	P4	D5	P5	m6

Key of D♯ M6

D♯	E	F	F♯	G	G♯	A	A♯	B	C	C♯	D	D♯	E	F	F♯	G	G♯	A	A♯	B	C	C♯	D	D♯
12	**11**	**10**	**9**	**8**	**7**	**6**	**5**	**4**	**3**	**2**	**1**	**0**	**1**	**2**	**3**	**4**	**5**	**6**	**7**	**8**	**9**	**10**	**11**	**12**
M6	m7	M7	OC	m2	M2	m3	M3	P4	D5	P5	m6	M6	m7	M7	OC	m2	M2	m3	M3	P4	D5	P5	m6	M6

Key of D♯ m7

D♯	E	F	F♯	G	G♯	A	A♯	B	C	C♯	D	D♯	E	F	F♯	G	G♯	A	A♯	B	C	C♯	D	D♯
12	11	10	9	8	7	6	5	4	3	2	1	0	1	2	3	4	5	6	7	8	9	10	11	12
	M7	OC		M2		M3	P4		P5		M6		M7	OC		M2		M3	P4		P5		M6	
m7			m2		m3			D5		m6		m7			m2		m3			D5		m6		m7

Key of D♯ M7

D♯	E	F	F♯	G	G♯	A	A♯	B	C	C♯	D	D♯	E	F	F♯	G	G♯	A	A♯	B	C	C♯	D	D♯
12	11	10	9	8	7	6	5	4	3	2	1	0	1	2	3	4	5	6	7	8	9	10	11	12
M7	OC		M2		M3	P4		P5		M6		M7	OC		M2		M3	P4		P5		M6		M7
		m2		m3			D5		m6		m7			m2		m3			D5		m6		m7	

Key of E (OC)

E	F	F♯	G	G♯	A	A♯	B	C	C♯	D	D♯	E	F	F♯	G	G♯	A	A♯	B	C	C♯	D	D♯	E
12	11	10	9	8	7	6	5	4	3	2	1	0	1	2	3	4	5	6	7	8	9	10	11	12
OC		M2		M3	P4		P5		M6		M7	OC		M2		M3	P4		P5		M6		M7	OC
	m2		m3			D5		m6		m7			m2		m3			D5		m6		m7		

Key of E m2

E	F	F♯	G	G♯	A	A♯	B	C	C♯	D	D♯	E	F	F♯	G	G♯	A	A♯	B	C	C♯	D	D♯	E
12	11	10	9	8	7	6	5	4	3	2	1	0	1	2	3	4	5	6	7	8	9	10	11	12
	M2		M3	P4		P5		M6		M7	OC		M2		M3	P4		P5		M6		M7	OC	
m2		m3			D5		m6		m7			m2		m3			D5		m6		m7			m2

Key of E M2

E	F	F♯	G	G♯	A	A♯	B	C	C♯	D	D♯	E	F	F♯	G	G♯	A	A♯	B	C	C♯	D	D♯	E
12	11	10	9	8	7	6	5	4	3	2	1	0	1	2	3	4	5	6	7	8	9	10	11	12
M2		M3	P4		P5		M6		M7	OC		M2		M3	P4		P5		M6		M7	OC		M2
	m3			D5		m6		m7			m2		m3			D5		m6		m7			m2	

Key of E m3

E	F	F♯	G	G♯	A	A♯	B	C	C♯	D	D♯	E	F	F♯	G	G♯	A	A♯	B	C	C♯	D	D♯	E
12	11	10	9	8	7	6	5	4	3	2	1	0	1	2	3	4	5	6	7	8	9	10	11	12
	M3	P4		P5		M6		M7	OC		M2		M3	P4		P5		M6		M7	OC		M2	
m3			D5		m6		m7			m2		m3			D5		m6		m7			m2		m3

Key of E M3

E	F	F♯	G	G♯	A	A♯	B	C	C♯	D	D♯	E	F	F♯	G	G♯	A	A♯	B	C	C♯	D	D♯	E
12	11	10	9	8	7	6	5	4	3	2	1	0	1	2	3	4	5	6	7	8	9	10	11	12
M3	P4		P5		M6		M7	OC		M2		M3	P4		P5		M6		M7	OC		M2		M3
		D5		m6		m7			m2		m3			D5		m6		m7			m2		m3	

Key of E P4

E	F	F♯	G	G♯	A	A♯	B	C	C♯	D	D♯	E	F	F♯	G	G♯	A	A♯	B	C	C♯	D	D♯	E
12	11	10	9	8	7	6	5	4	3	2	1	0	1	2	3	4	5	6	7	8	9	10	11	12
P4		P5		M6		M7	OC		M2		M3	P4		P5		M6		M7	OC		M2		M3	P4
	D5		m6		m7			m2		m3			D5		m6		m7			m2		m3		

Key of E D5

E	F	F♯	G	G♯	A	A♯	B	C	C♯	D	D♯	E	F	F♯	G	G♯	A	A♯	B	C	C♯	D	D♯	E
12	11	10	9	8	7	6	5	4	3	2	1	0	1	2	3	4	5	6	7	8	9	10	11	12
	P5		M6		M7	OC		M2		M3	P4		P5		M6		M7	OC		M2		M3	P4	
D5		m6		m7			m2		m3			D5		m6		m7			m2		m3			D5

Key of E P5

E	F	F♯	G	G♯	A	A♯	B	C	C♯	D	D♯	E	F	F♯	G	G♯	A	A♯	B	C	C♯	D	D♯	E
12	11	10	9	8	7	6	5	4	3	2	1	0	1	2	3	4	5	6	7	8	9	10	11	12
P5		M6		M7	OC		M2		M3	P4		P5		M6		M7	OC		M2		M3	P4		P5
	m6		m7			m2		m3			D5		m6		m7			m2		m3			D5	

Key of E m6

E	F	F♯	G	G♯	A	A♯	B	C	C♯	D	D♯	E	F	F♯	G	G♯	A	A♯	B	C	C♯	D	D♯	E
12	11	10	9	8	7	6	5	4	3	2	1	0	1	2	3	4	5	6	7	8	9	10	11	12
	M6		M7	OC		M2		M3	P4		P5		M6		M7	OC		M2		M3	P4		P5	
m6		m7			m2		m3			D5		m6		m7			m2		m3			D5		m6

Key of E M6

E	F	F♯	G	G♯	A	A♯	B	C	C♯	D	D♯	E	F	F♯	G	G♯	A	A♯	B	C	C♯	D	D♯	E
12	11	10	9	8	7	6	5	4	3	2	1	0	1	2	3	4	5	6	7	8	9	10	11	12
M6		M7	OC		M2		M3	P4		P5		M6		M7	OC		M2		M3	P4		P5		M6
	m7			m2		m3			D5		m6		m7			m2		m3			D5		m6	

Key of E m7

E	F	F♯	G	G♯	A	A♯	B	C	C♯	D	D♯	E	F	F♯	G	G♯	A	A♯	B	C	C♯	D	D♯	E
12	11	10	9	8	7	6	5	4	3	2	1	0	1	2	3	4	5	6	7	8	9	10	11	12
	M7	OC		M2		M3	P4		P5		M6		M7	OC		M2		M3	P4		P5		M6	
m7			m2		m3			D5		m6		m7			m2		m3			D5		m6		m7

Key of E M7

E	F	F♯	G	G♯	A	A♯	B	C	C♯	D	D♯	E	F	F♯	G	G♯	A	A♯	B	C	C♯	D	D♯	E
12	11	10	9	8	7	6	5	4	3	2	1	0	1	2	3	4	5	6	7	8	9	10	11	12
M7	OC		M2		M3	P4		P5		M6		M7	OC		M2		M3	P4		P5		M6		M7
		m2		m3			D5		m6		m7			m2		m3			D5		m6		m7	

Key of F (OC)

F	F♯	G	G♯	A	A♯	B	C	C♯	D	D♯	E	F	F♯	G	G♯	A	A♯	B	C	C♯	D	D♯	E	F
12	11	10	9	8	7	6	5	4	3	2	1	0	1	2	3	4	5	6	7	8	9	10	11	12
OC		M2		M3	P4		P5		M6		M7	OC		M2		M3	P4		P5		M6		M7	OC
	m2		m3			D5		m6		m7			m2		m3			D5		m6		m7		

Key of F m2

F	F♯	G	G♯	A	A♯	B	C	C♯	D	D♯	E	F	F♯	G	G♯	A	A♯	B	C	C♯	D	D♯	E	F
12	11	10	9	8	7	6	5	4	3	2	1	0	1	2	3	4	5	6	7	8	9	10	11	12
	M2		M3	P4		P5		M6		M7	OC		M2		M3	P4		P5		M6		M7	OC	
m2		m3			D5		m6		m7			m2		m3			D5		m6		m7			m2

Key of F M2

F	F♯	G	G♯	A	A♯	B	C	C♯	D	D♯	E	F	F♯	G	G♯	A	A♯	B	C	C♯	D	D♯	E	F
12	11	10	9	8	7	6	5	4	3	2	1	0	1	2	3	4	5	6	7	8	9	10	11	12
M2		M3	P4		P5		M6		M7	OC		M2		M3	P4		P5		M6		M7	OC		M2
	m3			D5		m6		m7			m2		m3			D5		m6		m7			m2	

Key of F m3

F	F♯	G	G♯	A	A♯	B	C	C♯	D	D♯	E	F	F♯	G	G♯	A	A♯	B	C	C♯	D	D♯	E	F
12	11	10	9	8	7	6	5	4	3	2	1	0	1	2	3	4	5	6	7	8	9	10	11	12
	M3	P4		P5		M6		M7	OC		M2		M3	P4		P5		M6		M7	OC		M2	
m3			D5		m6		m7			m2		m3			D5		m6		m7			m2		m3

Key of F M3

F	F♯	G	G♯	A	A♯	B	C	C♯	D	D♯	E	F	F♯	G	G♯	A	A♯	B	C	C♯	D	D♯	E	F
12	11	10	9	8	7	6	5	4	3	2	1	0	1	2	3	4	5	6	7	8	9	10	11	12
M3	P4		P5		M6		M7	OC		M2		M3	P4		P5		M6		M7	OC		M2		M3
		D5		m6		m7			m2		m3			D5		m6		m7			m2		m3	

Key of F P4

F	F♯	G	G♯	A	A♯	B	C	C♯	D	D♯	E	F	F♯	G	G♯	A	A♯	B	C	C♯	D	D♯	E	F
12	11	10	9	8	7	6	5	4	3	2	1	0	1	2	3	4	5	6	7	8	9	10	11	12
P4		P5		M6		M7	OC		M2		M3	P4		P5		M6		M7	OC		M2		M3	P4
	D5		m6		m7			m2		m3			D5		m6		m7			m2		m3		

Key of F D5

F	F♯	G	G♯	A	A♯	B	C	C♯	D	D♯	E	F	F♯	G	G♯	A	A♯	B	C	C♯	D	D♯	E	F
12	11	10	9	8	7	6	5	4	3	2	1	0	1	2	3	4	5	6	7	8	9	10	11	12
	P5		M6		M7	OC		M2		M3	P4		P5		M6		M7	OC		M2		M3	P4	
D5		m6		m7			m2		m3			D5		m6		m7			m2		m3			D5

Key of F P5

F	F♯	G	G♯	A	A♯	B	C	C♯	D	D♯	E	F	F♯	G	G♯	A	A♯	B	C	C♯	D	D♯	E	F
12	11	10	9	8	7	6	5	4	3	2	1	0	1	2	3	4	5	6	7	8	9	10	11	12
P5		M6		M7	OC		M2		M3	P4		P5		M6		M7	OC		M2		M3	P4		P5
	m6		m7			m2		m3			D5		m6		m7			m2		m3			D5	

Key of F m6

F	F♯	G	G♯	A	A♯	B	C	C♯	D	D♯	E	F	F♯	G	G♯	A	A♯	B	C	C♯	D	D♯	E	F
12	11	10	9	8	7	6	5	4	3	2	1	0	1	2	3	4	5	6	7	8	9	10	11	12
	M6		M7	OC		M2		M3	P4		P5		M6		M7	OC		M2		M3	P4		P5	
m6		m7			m2		m3			D5		m6		m7			m2		m3			D5		m6

Key of F M6

F	F♯	G	G♯	A	A♯	B	C	C♯	D	D♯	E	F	F♯	G	G♯	A	A♯	B	C	C♯	D	D♯	E	F
12	11	10	9	8	7	6	5	4	3	2	1	0	1	2	3	4	5	6	7	8	9	10	11	12
M6		M7	OC		M2		M3	P4		P5		M6		M7	OC		M2		M3	P4		P5		M6
	m7			m2		m3			D5		m6		m7			m2		m3			D5		m6	

Key of F m7

F	F♯	G	G♯	A	A♯	B	C	C♯	D	D♯	E	F	F♯	G	G♯	A	A♯	B	C	C♯	D	D♯	E	F
12	11	10	9	8	7	6	5	4	3	2	1	0	1	2	3	4	5	6	7	8	9	10	11	12
	M7	OC		M2		M3	P4		P5		M6		M7	OC		M2		M3	P4		P5		M6	
m7			m2		m3			D5		m6		m7			m2		m3			D5		m6		m7

Key of F M7

F	F♯	G	G♯	A	A♯	B	C	C♯	D	D♯	E	F	F♯	G	G♯	A	A♯	B	C	C♯	D	D♯	E	F
12	11	10	9	8	7	6	5	4	3	2	1	0	1	2	3	4	5	6	7	8	9	10	11	12
M7	OC		M2		M3	P4		P5		M6		M7	OC		M2		M3	P4		P5		M6		M7
		m2		m3			D5		m6		m7			m2		m3			D5		m6		m7	

Key of F♯ (OC)

F♯	G	G♯	A	A♯	B	C	C♯	D	D♯	E	F	F♯	G	G♯	A	A♯	B	C	C♯	D	D♯	E	F	F♯
12	11	10	9	8	7	6	5	4	3	2	1	0	1	2	3	4	5	6	7	8	9	10	11	12
OC		M2		M3	P4		P5		M6		M7	OC		M2		M3	P4		P5		M6		M7	OC
	m2		m3			D5		m6		m7			m2		m3			D5		m6		m7		

Key of F♯ m2

F♯	G	G♯	A	A♯	B	C	C♯	D	D♯	E	F	F♯	G	G♯	A	A♯	B	C	C♯	D	D♯	E	F	F♯
12	11	10	9	8	7	6	5	4	3	2	1	0	1	2	3	4	5	6	7	8	9	10	11	12
	M2		M3	P4		P5		M6		M7	OC		M2		M3	P4		P5		M6		M7	OC	
m2		m3			D5		m6		m7			m2		m3			D5		m6		m7			m2

Key of F♯ M2

F♯	G	G♯	A	A♯	B	C	C♯	D	D♯	E	F	F♯	G	G♯	A	A♯	B	C	C♯	D	D♯	E	F	F♯
12	11	10	9	8	7	6	5	4	3	2	1	0	1	2	3	4	5	6	7	8	9	10	11	12
M2		M3	P4		P5		M6		M7	OC		M2		M3	P4		P5		M6		M7	OC		M2
	m3			D5		m6		m7			m2		m3			D5		m6		m7			m2	

Key of F♯ m3

F♯	G	G♯	A	A♯	B	C	C♯	D	D♯	E	F	F♯	G	G♯	A	A♯	B	C	C♯	D	D♯	E	F	F♯
12	11	10	9	8	7	6	5	4	3	2	1	0	1	2	3	4	5	6	7	8	9	10	11	12
	M3	P4		P5		M6		M7	OC		M2		M3	P4		P5		M6		M7	OC		M2	
m3			D5		m6		m7			m2		m3			D5		m6		m7			m2		m3

Key of F♯ M3

F♯	G	G♯	A	A♯	B	C	C♯	D	D♯	E	F	F♯	G	G♯	A	A♯	B	C	C♯	D	D♯	E	F	F♯
12	11	10	9	8	7	6	5	4	3	2	1	0	1	2	3	4	5	6	7	8	9	10	11	12
M3	P4	D5	P5	m6	M6	m7	M7	OC	m2	M2	m3	M3	P4	D5	P5	m6	M6	m7	M7	OC	m2	M2	m3	M3

Key of F♯ P4

F♯	G	G♯	A	A♯	B	C	C♯	D	D♯	E	F	F♯	G	G♯	A	A♯	B	C	C♯	D	D♯	E	F	F♯
12	11	10	9	8	7	6	5	4	3	2	1	0	1	2	3	4	5	6	7	8	9	10	11	12
P4	D5	P5	m6	M6	m7	M7	OC	m2	M2	m3	M3	P4	D5	P5	m6	M6	m7	M7	OC	m2	M2	m3	M3	P4

Key of F♯ D5

F♯	G	G♯	A	A♯	B	C	C♯	D	D♯	E	F	F♯	G	G♯	A	A♯	B	C	C♯	D	D♯	E	F	F♯
12	11	10	9	8	7	6	5	4	3	2	1	0	1	2	3	4	5	6	7	8	9	10	11	12
D5	P5	m6	M6	m7	M7	OC	m2	M2	m3	M3	P4	D5	P5	m6	M6	m7	M7	OC	m2	M2	m3	M3	P4	D5

Key of F♯ P5

F♯	G	G♯	A	A♯	B	C	C♯	D	D♯	E	F	F♯	G	G♯	A	A♯	B	C	C♯	D	D♯	E	F	F♯
12	11	10	9	8	7	6	5	4	3	2	1	0	1	2	3	4	5	6	7	8	9	10	11	12
P5	m6	M6	m7	M7	OC	m2	M2	m3	M3	P4	D5	P5	m6	M6	m7	M7	OC	m2	M2	m3	M3	P4	D5	P5

Key of F♯ m6

F♯	G	G♯	A	A♯	B	C	C♯	D	D♯	E	F	F♯	G	G♯	A	A♯	B	C	C♯	D	D♯	E	F	F♯
12	11	10	9	8	7	6	5	4	3	2	1	0	1	2	3	4	5	6	7	8	9	10	11	12
m6	M6	m7	M7	OC	m2	M2	m3	M3	P4	D5	P5	m6	M6	m7	M7	OC	m2	M2	m3	M3	P4	D5	P5	m6

Key of F♯ M6

F♯	G	G♯	A	A♯	B	C	C♯	D	D♯	E	F	F♯	G	G♯	A	A♯	B	C	C♯	D	D♯	E	F	F♯
12	11	10	9	8	7	6	5	4	3	2	1	0	1	2	3	4	5	6	7	8	9	10	11	12
M6	m7	M7	OC	m2	M2	m3	M3	P4	D5	P5	m6	M6	m7	M7	OC	m2	M2	m3	M3	P4	D5	P5	m6	M6

Key of F♯ m7

F♯	G	G♯	A	A♯	B	C	C♯	D	D♯	E	F	F♯	G	G♯	A	A♯	B	C	C♯	D	D♯	E	F	F♯
12	11	10	9	8	7	6	5	4	3	2	1	0	1	2	3	4	5	6	7	8	9	10	11	12
m7	M7	OC	m2	M2	m3	M3	P4	D5	P5	m6	M6	m7	M7	OC	m2	M2	m3	M3	P4	D5	P5	m6	M6	m7

Key of F♯ M7

F♯	G	G♯	A	A♯	B	C	C♯	D	D♯	E	F	F♯	G	G♯	A	A♯	B	C	C♯	D	D♯	E	F	F♯
12	11	10	9	8	7	6	5	4	3	2	1	0	1	2	3	4	5	6	7	8	9	10	11	12
M7	OC	m2	M2	m3	M3	P4	D5	P5	m6	M6	m7	M7	OC	m2	M2	m3	M3	P4	D5	P5	m6	M6	m7	M7

Key of G (OC)

G	G♯	A	A♯	B	C	C♯	D	D♯	E	F	F♯	G	G♯	A	A♯	B	C	C♯	D	D♯	E	F	F♯	G
12	11	10	9	8	7	6	5	4	3	2	1	0	1	2	3	4	5	6	7	8	9	10	11	12
OC	m2	M2	m3	M3	P4	D5	P5	m6	M6	m7	M7	OC	m2	M2	m3	M3	P4	D5	P5	m6	M6	m7	M7	OC

Key of G m2

G	G♯	A	A♯	B	C	C♯	D	D♯	E	F	F♯	G	G♯	A	A♯	B	C	C♯	D	D♯	E	F	F♯	G
12	11	10	9	8	7	6	5	4	3	2	1	0	1	2	3	4	5	6	7	8	9	10	11	12
m2	M2	m3	M3	P4	D5	P5	m6	M6	m7	M7	OC	m2	M2	m3	M3	P4	D5	P5	m6	M6	m7	M7	OC	m2

Key of G M2

G	G♯	A	A♯	B	C	C♯	D	D♯	E	F	F♯	G	G♯	A	A♯	B	C	C♯	D	D♯	E	F	F♯	G
12	11	10	9	8	7	6	5	4	3	2	1	0	1	2	3	4	5	6	7	8	9	10	11	12
M2	m3	M3	P4	D5	P5	m6	M6	m7	M7	OC	m2	M2	m3	M3	P4	D5	P5	m6	M6	m7	M7	OC	m2	M2

Key of G m3

G	G♯	A	A♯	B	C	C♯	D	D♯	E	F	F♯	G	G♯	A	A♯	B	C	C♯	D	D♯	E	F	F♯	G
12	11	10	9	8	7	6	5	4	3	2	1	0	1	2	3	4	5	6	7	8	9	10	11	12
m3	M3	P4	D5	P5	m6	M6	m7	M7	OC	m2	M2	m3	M3	P4	D5	P5	m6	M6	m7	M7	OC	m2	M2	m3

Key of G M3

G	G♯	A	A♯	B	C	C♯	D	D♯	E	F	F♯	G	G♯	A	A♯	B	C	C♯	D	D♯	E	F	F♯	G
12	11	10	9	8	7	6	5	4	3	2	1	0	1	2	3	4	5	6	7	8	9	10	11	12
M3	P4		P5		M6		M7	OC		M2		M3	P4		P5		M6		M7	OC		M2		M3
		D5		m6		m7			m2		m3			D5		m6		m7			m2		m3	

Key of G P4

G	G♯	A	A♯	B	C	C♯	D	D♯	E	F	F♯	G	G♯	A	A♯	B	C	C♯	D	D♯	E	F	F♯	G
12	11	10	9	8	7	6	5	4	3	2	1	0	1	2	3	4	5	6	7	8	9	10	11	12
P4		P5		M6		M7	OC		M2		M3	P4		P5		M6		M7	OC		M2		M3	P4
	D5		m6		m7			m2		m3			D5		m6		m7			m2		m3		

Key of G D5

G	G♯	A	A♯	B	C	C♯	D	D♯	E	F	F♯	G	G♯	A	A♯	B	C	C♯	D	D♯	E	F	F♯	G
12	11	10	9	8	7	6	5	4	3	2	1	0	1	2	3	4	5	6	7	8	9	10	11	12
	P5		M6		M7	OC		M2		M3	P4		P5		M6		M7	OC		M2		M3	P4	
D5		m6		m7			m2		m3			D5		m6		m7			m2		m3			D5

Key of G P5

G	G♯	A	A♯	B	C	C♯	D	D♯	E	F	F♯	G	G♯	A	A♯	B	C	C♯	D	D♯	E	F	F♯	G
12	11	10	9	8	7	6	5	4	3	2	1	0	1	2	3	4	5	6	7	8	9	10	11	12
P5		M6		M7	OC		M2		M3	P4		P5		M6		M7	OC		M2		M3	P4		P5
	m6		m7			m2		m3			D5		m6		m7			m2		m3			D5	

Key of G m6

G	G♯	A	A♯	B	C	C♯	D	D♯	E	F	F♯	G	G♯	A	A♯	B	C	C♯	D	D♯	E	F	F♯	G
12	11	10	9	8	7	6	5	4	3	2	1	0	1	2	3	4	5	6	7	8	9	10	11	12
	M6		M7	OC		M2		M3	P4		P5		M6		M7	OC		M2		M3	P4		P5	
m6		m7			m2		m3			D5		m6		m7			m2		m3			D5		m6

Key of G M6

G	G♯	A	A♯	B	C	C♯	D	D♯	E	F	F♯	G	G♯	A	A♯	B	C	C♯	D	D♯	E	F	F♯	G
12	11	10	9	8	7	6	5	4	3	2	1	0	1	2	3	4	5	6	7	8	9	10	11	12
M6		M7	OC		M2		M3	P4		P5		M6		M7	OC		M2		M3	P4		P5		M6
	m7			m2		m3			D5		m6		m7			m2		m3			D5		m6	

Key of G m7

G	G♯	A	A♯	B	C	C♯	D	D♯	E	F	F♯	G	G♯	A	A♯	B	C	C♯	D	D♯	E	F	F♯	G
12	11	10	9	8	7	6	5	4	3	2	1	0	1	2	3	4	5	6	7	8	9	10	11	12
	M7	OC		M2		M3	P4		P5		M6		M7	OC		M2		M3	P4		P5		M6	
m7			m2		m3			D5		m6		m7			m2		m3			D5		m6		m7

Key of G M7

G	G♯	A	A♯	B	C	C♯	D	D♯	E	F	F♯	G	G♯	A	A♯	B	C	C♯	D	D♯	E	F	F♯	G
12	11	10	9	8	7	6	5	4	3	2	1	0	1	2	3	4	5	6	7	8	9	10	11	12
M7	OC		M2		M3	P4		P5		M6		M7	OC		M2		M3	P4		P5		M6		M7
		m2		m3			D5		m6		m7			m2		m3			D5		m6		m7	

Key of G♯ (OC)

G♯	A	A♯	B	C	C♯	D	D♯	E	F	F♯	G	G♯	A	A♯	B	C	C♯	D	D♯	E	F	F♯	G	G♯
12	11	10	9	8	7	6	5	4	3	2	1	0	1	2	3	4	5	6	7	8	9	10	11	12
OC		M2		M3	P4		P5		M6		M7	OC		M2		M3	P4		P5		M6		M7	OC
	m2		m3			D5		m6		m7			m2		m3			D5		m6		m7		

Key of G♯ m2

G♯	A	A♯	B	C	C♯	D	D♯	E	F	F♯	G	G♯	A	A♯	B	C	C♯	D	D♯	E	F	F♯	G	G♯
12	11	10	9	8	7	6	5	4	3	2	1	0	1	2	3	4	5	6	7	8	9	10	11	12
	M2		M3	P4		P5		M6		M7	OC		M2		M3	P4		P5		M6		M7	OC	
m2		m3			D5		m6		m7			m2		m3			D5		m6		m7			m2

Key of G♯ M2

G♯	A	A♯	B	C	C♯	D	D♯	E	F	F♯	G	G♯	A	A♯	B	C	C♯	D	D♯	E	F	F♯	G	G♯
12	11	10	9	8	7	6	5	4	3	2	1	0	1	2	3	4	5	6	7	8	9	10	11	12
M2		M3	P4		P5		M6		M7	OC		M2		M3	P4		P5		M6		M7	OC		M2
	m3			D5		m6		m7			m2		m3			D5		m6		m7			m2	

Key of G♯ m3

G♯	A	A♯	B	C	C♯	D	D♯	E	F	F♯	G	G♯	A	A♯	B	C	C♯	D	D♯	E	F	F♯	G	G♯
12	11	10	9	8	7	6	5	4	3	2	1	0	1	2	3	4	5	6	7	8	9	10	11	12
	M3	P4		P5		M6		M7	OC		M2		M3	P4		P5		M6		M7	OC		M2	
m3			D5		m6		m7			m2		m3			D5		m6		m7			m2		m3

Key of G♯ M3

G♯	A	A♯	B	C	C♯	D	D♯	E	F	F♯	G	G♯	A	A♯	B	C	C♯	D	D♯	E	F	F♯	G	G♯
12	11	10	9	8	7	6	5	4	3	2	1	0	1	2	3	4	5	6	7	8	9	10	11	12
M3	P4		P5		M6		M7	OC		M2		M3	P4		P5		M6		M7	OC		M2		M3
		D5		m6		m7			m2		m3			D5		m6		m7			m2		m3	

Key of G♯ P4

G♯	A	A♯	B	C	C♯	D	D♯	E	F	F♯	G	G♯	A	A♯	B	C	C♯	D	D♯	E	F	F♯	G	G♯
12	11	10	9	8	7	6	5	4	3	2	1	0	1	2	3	4	5	6	7	8	9	10	11	12
P4		P5		M6		M7	OC		M2		M3	P4		P5		M6		M7	OC		M2		M3	P4
	D5		m6		m7			m2		m3			D5		m6		m7			m2		m3		

Key of G♯ D5

G♯	A	A♯	B	C	C♯	D	D♯	E	F	F♯	G	G♯	A	A♯	B	C	C♯	D	D♯	E	F	F♯	G	G♯
12	11	10	9	8	7	6	5	4	3	2	1	0	1	2	3	4	5	6	7	8	9	10	11	12
	P5		M6		M7	OC		M2		M3	P4		P5		M6		M7	OC		M2		M3	P4	
D5		m6		m7			m2		m3			D5		m6		m7			m2		m3			D5

Key of G♯ P5

G♯	A	A♯	B	C	C♯	D	D♯	E	F	F♯	G	G♯	A	A♯	B	C	C♯	D	D♯	E	F	F♯	G	G♯
12	11	10	9	8	7	6	5	4	3	2	1	0	1	2	3	4	5	6	7	8	9	10	11	12
P5		M6		M7	OC		M2		M3	P4		P5		M6		M7	OC		M2		M3	P4		P5
	m6		m7			m2		m3			D5		m6		m7			m2		m3			D5	

Key of G♯ m6

G♯	A	A♯	B	C	C♯	D	D♯	E	F	F♯	G	G♯	A	A♯	B	C	C♯	D	D♯	E	F	F♯	G	G♯
12	11	10	9	8	7	6	5	4	3	2	1	0	1	2	3	4	5	6	7	8	9	10	11	12
	M6		M7	OC		M2		M3	P4		P5		M6		M7	OC		M2		M3	P4		P5	
m6		m7			m2		m3			D5		m6		m7			m2		m3			D5		m6

Key of G♯ M6

G♯	A	A♯	B	C	C♯	D	D♯	E	F	F♯	G	G♯	A	A♯	B	C	C♯	D	D♯	E	F	F♯	G	G♯
12	11	10	9	8	7	6	5	4	3	2	1	0	1	2	3	4	5	6	7	8	9	10	11	12
M6		M7	OC		M2		M3	P4		P5		M6		M7	OC		M2		M3	P4		P5		M6
	m7			m2		m3			D5		m6		m7			m2		m3			D5		m6	

Key of G♯ m7

G♯	A	A♯	B	C	C♯	D	D♯	E	F	F♯	G	G♯	A	A♯	B	C	C♯	D	D♯	E	F	F♯	G	G♯
12	11	10	9	8	7	6	5	4	3	2	1	0	1	2	3	4	5	6	7	8	9	10	11	12
	M7	OC		M2		M3	P4		P5		M6		M7	OC		M2		M3	P4		P5		M6	
m7			m2		m3			D5		m6		m7			m2		m3			D5		m6		m7

Key of G♯ M7

G♯	A	A♯	B	C	C♯	D	D♯	E	F	F♯	G	G♯	A	A♯	B	C	C♯	D	D♯	E	F	F♯	G	G♯
12	11	10	9	8	7	6	5	4	3	2	1	0	1	2	3	4	5	6	7	8	9	10	11	12
M7	OC		M2		M3	P4		P5		M6		M7	OC		M2		M3	P4		P5		M6		M7
		m2		m3			D5		m6		m7			m2		m3			D5		m6		m7	

Interval - Scale Compatibility

Scale-Sets

m2

5 Tone Scales

Iwato	1	♭2			4	♭5				♭7
Japanese (a)	1	♭2			4		5	♭6		
Japanese (in sen)	1	♭2			4		5			♭7
Kumoi 2	1	♭2			4		5	♭6		
Pelog	1	♭2	♭3				5	♭6		
Pelog 2	1	♭2	♭3				5			♭7

6 Tone Scales

Prometheus Neopolitan	1	♭2		3		♭5			6	♭7
Six Tone Symmetrical	1	♭2		3	4			♯5	6	

7 Tone Scales

Altered	1	♭2	♭3	♭4		♭5		♭6		♭7

Byzantine	1	♭2			3	4		5	♭6			7
Diminished Whole Tone	1	♭2		♭3	3		♭5		♭6		♭7	
Double Harmonic	1	♭2			3	4		5	♭6			7
Enigmatic	1	♭2			3		♯4		♯5		♯6	7
Hungarian Gypsy Persian	1	♭2			3	4		5	♭6			7
Javanese	1	♭2		♭3		4		5		6	♭7	
Locrian	1	♭2		♭3		4	♭5		♭6		♭7	
Locrian 6	1	♭2		♭3		4	♭5			6	♭7	
Super Locrian	1	♭2		♯2	3		♯4		♯5		♭7	
Ultra Locrian	1	♭2		♭3	3		♭5		♭6	6		
Neopolitan	1	♭2		♭3		4		5	♭6			7
Neopolitan Major	1	♭2		♭3		4		5		6		7
Neopolitan Minor	1	♭2		♭3		4		5	♭6		♭7	
Oriental (a)	1	♭2			3	4	♭5		♭6		♭7	
Oriental (b)	1	♭2			3	4	♭5			6	♭7	
Persian	1	♭2			3	4	♭5		♭6			7
Phrygian	1	♭2		♭3		4		5	♭6		♭7	
Phrygian Major	1	♭2			3	4		5	♭6		♭7	
Spanish Gypsy	1	♭2			3	4		5	♭6		♭7	

8 Tone Scales

Auxiliary Diminished Blues	1	♭2		♭3	3		♭5	5		6	♭7	
Bebop Half-Diminished	1	♭2		♭3		4	♭5	5	♭6			7
Eight Tone Spanish	1	♭2		♯2	3	4	♭5		♭6		♭7	
Jewish (Adonai Malakh)	1	♭2	2	♭3		4		5		6	♭7	
Jewish (Magen Abot)	1	♭2		♯2	3		♯4		♯5		♯6	7
Octatonic (H-W)	1	♭2		♭3	3		♭5	5		6	♭7	

9 Tone Scales

Moorish Phrygian	1	♭2		♭3	3	4		5	♯5		♭7	7

M2

5 Tone Scales

Chinese 2	1		2			4		5		6		
Dominant Pentatonic	1		2		3			5			♭7	
Hirajoshi	1		2	♭3				5	♭6			

Japanese (b)	1	2			4		5	b6			
Kumoi	1	2	b3				5		6		
Pentatonic Major	1	2		3			5		6		
Pentatonic Neutral	1	2			4		5			b7	

6 Tone Scales

Auxiliary Augmented	1	2		3		#4		#5		#6	
Major Blues Scale	1	2	b3	3			5		6		
Prometheus	1	2		3		b5			6	b7	
Whole Tone	1	2		3		#4		#5		b7	

7 Tone Scales

Aeolian	1	2	b3		4		5	b6		b7	
Arabian (b)	1	2		3	4	#4		#5		b7	
Dorian	1	2	b3		4		5		6	b7	
Dorian #4	1	2	b3			#4	5		6	b7	
Half Diminished #2	1	2	b3		4	b5		b6		b7	
Harmonic Minor	1	2	b3		4		5	b6			7
Hawaiian	1	2	b3		4		5		6		7
Hindu	1	2		3	4		5	b6		b7	
Hungarian Minor	1	2	b3			#4	5	b6			7
Ionian #5	1	2		3	4			#5	6		7
Leading Whole Tone	1	2		3		#4		#5		#6	7
Major Locrian	1	2		3	4	b5		b6		b7	
Lydian	1	2		3		#4	5		6		7
Lydian Minor	1	2		3		#4	5	b6		b7	
Lydian Augmented	1	2		3		#4		#5	6		7
Lydian Diminished	1	2	b3			#4	5		6		7
Major (Ionian)	1	2		3	4		5		6		7
Melodic Minor (ascending)	1	2	b3		4		5		6		7
Melodic Minor (descending)	1	2	b3		4		5	b6		b7	
Mixolydian	1	2		3	4		5		6	b7	
Overtone Dominant	1	2		3		#4	5		6	b7	
Roumanian Minor	1	2	b3			#4	5		6	b7	

8 Tone Scales

Algerian	1	2	b3	3	4	#4		b6			7
Arabian (a)	1	2	b3		4	#4		#5	6		7
Bebop Major	1	2		3	4		5	#5	6		7

Bebop Minor	1		2	♭3	3	4		5		6	♭7	
Bebop Dominant	1		2		3	4		5		6	♭7	7
Diminished	1		2	♭3		4	♭5		♭6	6		7
Japanese (Ichikosucho)	1		2		3	4	♯4	5		6		7
Jewish (Adonai Malakh)	1	♭2	2	♭3		4		5		6	♭7	
Octatonic (W-H)	1		2	♭3		4	♭5		♭6	6		7

9 Tone Scales

Japanese (Taishikcho)	1		2		3	4	♯4	5		6	♯6	7
Nine Tone Scale	1		2	♯2	3		♯4	5	♯5	6		7

m3

5 Tone Scales

Hirajoshi	1		2	♭3				5	♭6			
Kumoi	1		2	♭3				5		6		
Pelog	1	♭2		♭3				5	♭6			
Pelog 2	1	♭2		♭3				5			♭7	
Pentatonic Minor	1			♭3		4		5			♭7	

6 Tone Scales

Augmented	1			♯2	3		♯4		♯5			7
Blues	1			♭3		4	♯4	5			♭7	
Major Blues Scale	1		2	♭3	3			5		6		

7 Tone Scales

Aeolian	1		2	♭3		4		5	♭6		♭7	
Altered	1	♭2		♭3	♭4		♭5		♭6		♭7	
Blues Variation 1	1			♭3		4	♭5	5			♭7	7
Diminished Whole Tone	1	♭2		♭3	3		♭5		♭6		♭7	
Dorian	1		2	♭3		4		5		6	♭7	
Dorian ♯4	1		2	♭3			♯4	5		6	♭7	
Half Diminished ♯2	1		2	♭3		4	♭5		♭6		♭7	
Harmonic Minor	1		2	♭3		4		5	♭6			7
Hawaiian	1		2	♭3		4		5		6		7
Hungarian Major	1			♯2	3		♯4	5		6	♭7	

Hungarian Minor	1		2	♭3			♯4	5	♭6			7
Javanese	1	♭2		♭3		4		5		6	♭7	
Locrian	1	♭2		♭3		4	♭5		♭6		♭7	
Locrian 6	1	♭2		♭3		4	♭5			6	♭7	
Super Locrian	1	♭2		♯2	3		♯4		♯5		♭7	
Ultra Locrian	1	♭2		♭3	3		♭5		♭6	6		
Lydian Diminished	1		2	♭3			♯4	5		6		7
Lydian ♯2	1			♯2	3		♯4	5		6		7
Melodic Minor (ascending)	1		2	♭3		4		5		6		7
Melodic Minor (descending)	1		2	♭3		4		5	♭6		♭7	
Mixo-Blues	1			♭3	3	4	♭5	5			♭7	
Mohammedan	1			♭3	3	4		5	♭6	6		7
Neopolitan	1	♭2		♭3		4		5	♭6			7
Neopolitan Major	1	♭2		♭3		4		5		6		7
Neopolitan Minor	1	♭2		♭3		4		5	♭6		♭7	
Phrygian	1	♭2		♭3		4		5	♭6		♭7	
Roumanian Minor	1		2	♭3			♯4	5		6	♭7	

8 Tone Scales

Algerian	1		2	♭3	3	4	♯4		♭6			7
Arabian (a)	1		2	♭3		4	♯4		♯5	6		7
Auxiliary Diminished Blues	1	♭2		♭3	3		♭5	5		6	♭7	
Bebop Minor	1		2	♭3	3	4		5		6	♭7	
Bebop Half-Diminished	1	♭2		♭3		4	♭5	5	♭6			7
Blues Variation 2	1			♭3	3	4	♭5	5			♭7	7
Diminished	1		2	♭3		4	♭5		♭6	6		7
Eight Tone Spanish	1	♭2		♯2	3	4	♭5		♭6		♭7	
Jewish (Adonai Malakh)	1	♭2	2	♭3		4		5		6	♭7	
Jewish (Magen Abot)	1	♭2		♯2	3		♯4		♯5		♯6	7
Octatonic (H-W)	1	♭2		♭3	3		♭5	5		6	♭7	
Octatonic (W-H)	1		2	♭3		4	♭5		♭6	6		7

9 Tone Scales

Blues Variation 3	1			♭3	3	4	♭5	5		6	♭7	7
Moorish Phrygian	1	♭2		♭3	3	4		5	♯5		♭7	7
Nine Tone Scale	1		2	♯2	3		♯4	5	♯5	6		7

M3

5 Tone Scales

Chinese	1				3		♯4	5				7
Dominant Pentatonic	1		2		3			5			♭7	
Hirajoshi 2	1				3	4				6		7
Pentatonic Major	1		2		3			5		6		

6 Tone Scales

Augmented	1			♯2	3		♯4		♯5			7
Auxiliary Augmented	1		2		3		♯4		♯5		♯6	
Major Blues Scale	1		2	♭3	3			5		6		
Prometheus	1		2		3		♭5			6	♭7	
Prometheus Neopolitan	1	♭2			3		♭5			6	♭7	
Six Tone Symmetrical	1	♭2			3	4			♯5	6		
Whole Tone	1		2		3		♯4		♯5		♭7	

7 Tone Scales

Altered	1	♭2		♭3	♭4		♭5		♭6		♭7	
Arabian (b)	1		2		3	4	♯4		♯5		♭7	
Byzantine	1	♭2			3	4		5	♭6			7
Diminished Whole Tone	1	♭2		♭3	3		♭5		♭6		♭7	
Double Harmonic	1	♭2			3	4		5	♭6			7
Enigmatic	1	♭2			3		♯4		♯5		♯6	7
Hindu	1		2		3	4		5	♭6		♭7	
Hungarian Major	1			♯2	3		♯4	5		6	♭7	
Hungarian Gypsy Persian	1	♭2			3	4		5	♭6			7
Ionian ♯5	1		2		3	4			♯5	6		7
Leading Whole Tone	1		2		3		♯4		♯5		♯6	7
Major Locrian	1		2		3	4	♭5		♭6		♭7	
Super Locrian	1	♭2		♯2	3		♯4		♯5		♭7	
Ultra Locrian	1	♭2		♭3	3		♭5		♭6	6		
Lydian	1		2		3		♯4	5		6		7
Lydian Minor	1		2		3		♯4	5	♭6		♭7	
Lydian Augmented	1		2		3		♯4		♯5	6		7
Lydian ♯2	1			♯2	3		♯4	5		6		7
Major (Ionian)	1		2		3	4		5		6		7
Mixolydian	1		2		3	4		5		6	♭7	

Mixo-Blues	1			♭3	3	4	♭5	5			♭7	
Mohammedan	1			♭3	3	4		5	♭6	6		7
Oriental (a)	1	♭2			3	4	♭5		♭6		♭7	
Oriental (b)	1	♭2			3	4	♭5			6	♭7	
Overtone Dominant	1		2		3		♯4	5		6	♭7	
Persian	1	♭2			3	4	♭5		♭6			7
Phrygian Major	1	♭2			3	4		5	♭6		♭7	
Spanish Gypsy	1	♭2			3	4		5	♭6		♭7	

8 Tone Scales

Algerian	1		2	♭3	3	4	♯4		♭6			7
Auxiliary Diminished Blues	1	♭2		♭3	3		♭5	5		6	♭7	
Bebop Major	1		2		3	4		5	♯5	6		7
Bebop Minor	1		2	♭3	3	4		5		6	♭7	
Bebop Dominant	1		2		3	4		5		6	♭7	7
Blues Variation 2	1			♭3	3	4	♭5	5			♭7	7
Eight Tone Spanish	1	♭2		♯2	3	4	♭5		♭6		♭7	
Japanese (Ichikosucho)	1		2		3	4	♯4	5		6		7
Jewish (Magen Abot)	1	♭2		♯2	3		♯4		♯5		♯6	7
Octatonic (H-W)	1	♭2		♭3	3		♭5	5		6	♭7	

9 Tone Scales

Blues Variation 3	1			♭3	3	4	♭5	5		6	♭7	7
Japanese (Taishikcho)	1		2		3	4	♯4	5		6	♯6	7
Moorish Phrygian	1	♭2		♭3	3	4		5	♯5		♭7	7
Nine Tone Scale	1		2	♯2	3		♯4	5	♯5	6		7

P4

5 Tone Scales

Chinese 2	1		2			4		5		6		
Hirajoshi 2	1				3	4				6		7
Iwato	1	♭2				4	♭5				♭7	
Japanese (a)	1	♭2				4		5	♭6			
Japanese (b)	1		2			4		5	♭6			
Japanese (in sen)	1	♭2				4		5			♭7	
Kumoi 2	1	♭2				4		5	♭6			

Scale												
Pentatonic Neutral	1		2			4		5			♭7	
Pentatonic Minor	1			♭3		4		5			♭7	

6 Tone Scales

Scale												
Blues	1			♭3		4	♯4	5			♭7	
Six Tone Symmetrical	1	♭2			3	4			♯5	6		

7 Tone Scales

Scale												
Aeolian	1		2	♭3		4		5	♭6		♭7	
Arabian (b)	1		2		3	4	♯4		♯5		♭7	
Blues Variation 1	1			♭3		4	♭5	5			♭7	7
Byzantine	1	♭2			3	4		5	♭6			7
Dorian	1		2	♭3		4		5		6	♭7	
Double Harmonic	1	♭2			3	4		5	♭6			7
Half Diminished ♯2	1		2	♭3		4	♭5		♭6		♭7	
Harmonic Minor	1		2	♭3		4		5	♭6			7
Hawaiian	1		2	♭3		4		5		6		7
Hindu	1		2		3	4		5	♭6		♭7	
Hungarian Gypsy Persian	1	♭2			3	4		5	♭6			7
Ionian ♯5	1		2		3	4			♯5	6		7
Javanese	1	♭2		♭3		4		5		6	♭7	
Locrian	1	♭2		♭3		4	♭5		♭6		♭7	
Locrian 6	1	♭2		♭3		4	♭5			6	♭7	
Major Locrian	1		2		3	4	♭5		♭6		♭7	
Major (Ionian)	1		2		3	4		5		6		7
Melodic Minor (ascending)	1		2	♭3		4		5		6		7
Melodic Minor (descending)	1		2	♭3		4		5	♭6		♭7	
Mixolydian	1		2		3	4		5		6	♭7	
Mixo-Blues	1			♭3	3	4	♭5	5			♭7	
Mohammedan	1			♭3	3	4		5	♭6	6		7
Neopolitan	1	♭2		♭3		4		5	♭6			7
Neopolitan Major	1	♭2		♭3		4		5		6		7
Neopolitan Minor	1	♭2		♭3		4		5	♭6		♭7	
Oriental (a)	1	♭2			3	4	♭5		♭6		♭7	
Oriental (b)	1	♭2			3	4	♭5			6	♭7	
Persian	1	♭2			3	4	♭5		♭6			7
Phrygian	1	♭2		♭3		4		5	♭6		♭7	
Phrygian Major	1	♭2			3	4		5	♭6		♭7	
Spanish Gypsy	1	♭2			3	4		5	♭6		♭7	
	1	♭2	2	♭3	3	4	♭5	5	♭6	6	♭7	7

8 Tone Scales

Algerian	1		2	♭3	3	4	♯4		♭6			7
Arabian (a)	1		2	♭3		4	♯4		♯5	6		7
Bebop Major	1		2		3	4		5	♯5	6		7
Bebop Minor	1		2	♭3	3	4		5		6	♭7	
Bebop Dominant	1		2		3	4		5		6	♭7	7
Bebop Half-Diminished	1	♭2		♭3		4	♭5	5	♭6			7
Blues Variation 2	1			♭3	3	4	♭5	5			♭7	7
Diminished	1		2	♭3		4	♭5		♭6	6		7
Eight Tone Spanish	1	♭2		♯2	3	4	♭5		♭6		♭7	
Japanese (Ichikosucho)	1		2		3	4	♯4	5		6		7
Jewish (Adonai Malakh)	1	♭2	2	♭3		4		5		6	♭7	
Octatonic (W-H)	1		2	♭3		4	♭5		♭6	6		7

9 Tone Scales

Blues Variation 3	1			♭3	3	4	♭5	5		6	♭7	7
Japanese (Taishikcho)	1		2		3	4	♯4	5		6	♯6	7
Moorish Phrygian	1	♭2		♭3	3	4		5	♯5		♭7	7

D5

5 Tone Scales

Chinese	1				3		♯4	5				7
Iwato	1	♭2				4	♭5				♭7	

6 Tone Scales

Augmented	1			♯2	3		♯4		♯5			7
Auxiliary Augmented	1		2		3		♯4		♯5		♯6	
Blues	1			♭3		4	♯4	5			♭7	
Prometheus	1		2		3		♭5			6	♭7	
Prometheus Neopolitan	1	♭2			3		♭5			6	♭7	
Whole Tone	1		2		3		♯4		♯5		♭7	

7 Tone Scales

Altered	1	♭2		♭3	♭4		♭5		♭6		♭7	
Arabian (b)	1		2		3	4	♯4		♯5		♭7	

Blues Variation 1	1			♭3		4	♭5	5			♭7	7
Diminished Whole Tone	1	♭2		♭3	3		♭5		♭6		♭7	
Dorian ♯4	1		2	♭3			♯4	5		6	♭7	
Enigmatic	1	♭2			3		♯4		♯5		♯6	7
Half Diminished ♯2	1		2	♭3		4	♭5		♭6		♭7	
Hungarian Major	1			♯2	3		♯4	5		6	♭7	
Hungarian Minor	1		2	♭3			♯4	5	♭6			7
Leading Whole Tone	1		2		3		♯4		♯5		♯6	7
Locrian	1	♭2		♭3		4	♭5		♭6		♭7	
Locrian 6	1	♭2		♭3		4	♭5			6	♭7	
Major Locrian	1		2		3	4	♭5		♭6		♭7	
Super Locrian	1	♭2		♯2	3		♯4		♯5		♭7	
Ultra Locrian	1	♭2		♭3	3		♭5		♭6	6		
Lydian	1		2		3		♯4	5		6		7
Lydian Minor	1		2		3		♯4	5	♭6		♭7	
Lydian Augmented	1		2		3		♯4		♯5	6		7
Lydian Diminished	1		2	♭3			♯4	5		6		7
Lydian ♯2	1			♯2	3		♯4	5		6		7
Mixo-Blues	1			♭3	3	4	♭5	5			♭7	
Oriental (a)	1	♭2			3	4	♭5		♭6		♭7	
Oriental (b)	1	♭2			3	4	♭5			6	♭7	
Overtone Dominant	1		2		3		♯4	5		6	♭7	
Persian	1	♭2			3	4	♭5		♭6			7
Roumanian Minor	1		2	♭3			♯4	5		6	♭7	

8 Tone Scales

Algerian	1		2	♭3	3	4	♯4		♭6			7
Arabian (a)	1		2	♭3		4	♯4		♯5	6		7
Auxiliary Diminished Blues	1	♭2		♭3	3		♭5	5		6	♭7	
Bebop Half-Diminished	1	♭2		♭3		4	♭5	5	♭6			7
Blues Variation 2	1			♭3	3	4	♭5	5			♭7	7
Diminished	1		2	♭3		4	♭5		♭6	6		7
Eight Tone Spanish	1	♭2		♯2	3	4	♭5		♭6		♭7	
Japanese (Ichikosucho)	1		2		3	4	♯4	5		6		7
Jewish (Magen Abot)	1	♭2		♯2	3		♯4		♯5		♯6	7
Octatonic (H-W)	1	♭2		♭3	3		♭5	5		6	♭7	
Octatonic (W-H)	1		2	♭3		4	♭5		♭6	6		7
	1	♭2	2	♭3	3	4	♭5	5	♭6	6	♭7	7

9 Tone Scales

Blues Variation 3	1			♭3	3	4	♭5	5		6	♭7	7

Japanese (Taishikcho)	1		2		3	4	#4	5		6	#6	7
Nine Tone Scale	1		2	#2	3		#4	5	#5	6		7

P5

5 Tone Scales

Chinese	1				3		#4	5				7
Chinese 2	1		2			4		5		6		
Dominant Pentatonic	1		2		3			5			b7	
Hirajoshi	1		2	b3				5	b6			
Japanese (a)	1	b2				4		5	b6			
Japanese (b)	1		2			4		5	b6			
Japanese (in sen)	1	b2				4		5			b7	
Kumoi	1		2	b3				5		6		
Kumoi 2	1	b2				4		5	b6			
Pelog	1	b2		b3				5	b6			
Pelog 2	1	b2		b3				5			b7	
Pentatonic Major	1		2		3			5		6		
Pentatonic Neutral	1		2			4		5			b7	
Pentatonic Minor	1			b3		4		5			b7	

6 Tone Scales

Blues	1			b3		4	#4	5			b7	
Major Blues Scale	1		2	b3	3			5		6		

7 Tone Scales

Aeolian	1		2	b3		4		5	b6		b7	
Blues Variation 1	1			b3		4	b5	5			b7	7
Byzantine	1	b2			3	4		5	b6			7
Dorian	1		2	b3		4		5		6	b7	
Dorian #4	1		2	b3			#4	5		6	b7	
Double Harmonic	1	b2			3	4		5	b6			7
Harmonic Minor	1		2	b3		4		5	b6			7
Hawaiian	1		2	b3		4		5		6		7
Hindu	1		2		3	4		5	b6		b7	
Hungarian Major	1			#2	3		#4	5		6	b7	
Hungarian Minor	1		2	b3			#4	5	b6			7

Hungarian Gypsy Persian	1	♭2			3	4		5	♭6			7
Javanese	1	♭2		♭3		4		5		6	♭7	
Lydian	1		2		3		♯4	5		6		7
Lydian Minor	1		2		3		♯4	5	♭6		♭7	
Lydian Diminished	1		2	♭3			♯4	5		6		7
Lydian ♯2	1			♯2	3		♯4	5		6		7
Major (Ionian)	1		2		3	4		5		6		7
Melodic Minor (ascending)	1		2	♭3		4		5		6		7
Melodic Minor (descending)	1		2	♭3		4		5	♭6		♭7	
Mixolydian	1		2		3	4		5		6	♭7	
Mixo-Blues	1			♭3	3	4	♭5	5			♭7	
Mohammedan	1			♭3	3	4		5	♭6	6		7
Neopolitan	1	♭2		♭3		4		5	♭6			7
Neopolitan Major	1	♭2		♭3		4		5		6		7
Neopolitan Minor	1	♭2		♭3		4		5	♭6		♭7	
Overtone Dominant	1		2		3		♯4	5		6	♭7	
Phrygian	1	♭2		♭3		4		5	♭6		♭7	
Phrygian Major	1	♭2			3	4		5	♭6		♭7	
Roumanian Minor	1		2	♭3			♯4	5		6	♭7	
Spanish Gypsy	1	♭2			3	4		5	♭6		♭7	

8 Tone Scales

Auxiliary Diminished Blues	1	♭2		♭3	3		♭5	5		6	♭7	
Bebop Major	1		2		3	4		5	♯5	6		7
Bebop Minor	1		2	♭3	3	4		5		6	♭7	
Bebop Dominant	1		2		3	4		5		6	♭7	7
Bebop Half-Diminished	1	♭2		♭3		4	♭5	5	♭6			7
Blues Variation 2	1			♭3	3	4	♭5	5			♭7	7
Japanese (Ichikosucho)	1		2		3	4	♯4	5		6		7
Jewish (Adonai Malakh)	1	♭2	2	♭3		4		5		6	♭7	
Octatonic (H-W)	1	♭2		♭3	3		♭5	5		6	♭7	

9 Tone Scales

Blues Variation 3	1			♭3	3	4	♭5	5		6	♭7	7
Japanese (Taishikcho)	1		2		3	4	♯4	5		6	♯6	7
Moorish Phrygian	1	♭2		♭3	3	4		5	♯5		♭7	7
Nine Tone Scale	1		2	♯2	3		♯4	5	♯5	6		7

m6

5 Tone Scales

Hirajoshi	1		2	♭3				5	♭6			
Japanese (a)	1	♭2				4		5	♭6			
Japanese (b)	1		2			4		5	♭6			
Kumoi 2	1	♭2				4		5	♭6			
Pelog	1	♭2		♭3				5	♭6			

6 Tone Scales

Augmented	1			♯2	3		♯4		♯5			7
Auxiliary Augmented	1		2		3		♯4		♯5		♯6	
Six Tone Symmetrical	1	♭2			3	4			♯5	6		
Whole Tone	1		2		3		♯4		♯5		♭7	

7 Tone Scales

Aeolian	1		2	♭3		4		5	♭6		♭7	
Altered	1	♭2		♭3	♭4		♭5		♭6		♭7	
Arabian (b)	1		2		3	4	♯4		♯5		♭7	
Byzantine	1	♭2			3	4		5	♭6			7
Diminished Whole Tone	1	♭2		♭3	3		♭5		♭6		♭7	
Double Harmonic	1	♭2			3	4		5	♭6			7
Enigmatic	1	♭2			3		♯4		♯5		♯6	7
Half Diminished ♯2	1		2	♭3		4	♭5		♭6		♭7	
Harmonic Minor	1		2	♭3		4		5	♭6			7
Hindu	1		2		3	4		5	♭6		♭7	
Hungarian Minor	1		2	♭3			♯4	5	♭6			7
Hungarian Gypsy Persian	1	♭2			3	4		5	♭6			7
Ionian ♯5	1		2		3	4			♯5	6		7
Leading Whole Tone	1		2		3		♯4		♯5		♯6	7
Locrian	1	♭2		♭3		4	♭5		♭6		♭7	
Major Locrian	1		2		3	4	♭5		♭6		♭7	
Super Locrian	1	♭2		♯2	3		♯4		♯5		♭7	
Ultra Locrian	1	♭2		♭3	3		♭5		♭6	6		
Lydian Minor	1		2		3		♯4	5	♭6		♭7	
Lydian Augmented	1		2		3		♯4		♯5	6		7
Melodic Minor (descending)	1		2	♭3		4		5	♭6		♭7	
Mohammedan	1			♭3	3	4		5	♭6	6		7

Neopolitan	1	♭2		♭3		4		5	♭6			7
Neopolitan Minor	1	♭2		♭3		4		5	♭6		♭7	
Oriental (a)	1	♭2			3	4	♭5		♭6		♭7	
Persian	1	♭2			3	4	♭5		♭6			7
Phrygian	1	♭2		♭3		4		5	♭6		♭7	
Phrygian Major	1	♭2			3	4		5	♭6		♭7	
Spanish Gypsy	1	♭2			3	4		5	♭6		♭7	

8 Tone Scales

Algerian	1		2	♭3	3	4	♯4		♭6			7
Arabian (a)	1		2	♭3		4	♯4		♯5	6		7
Bebop Major	1		2		3	4		5	♯5	6		7
Bebop Half-Diminished	1	♭2		♭3		4	♭5	5	♭6			7
Diminished	1		2	♭3		4	♭5		♭6	6		7
Eight Tone Spanish	1	♭2		♯2	3	4	♭5		♭6		♭7	
Jewish (Magen Abot)	1	♭2		♯2	3		♯4		♯5		♯6	7
Octatonic (W-H)	1		2	♭3		4	♭5		♭6	6		7

9 Tone Scales

Moorish Phrygian	1	♭2		♭3	3	4		5	♯5		♭7	7
Nine Tone Scale	1		2	♯2	3		♯4	5	♯5	6		7

M6

5 Tone Scales

Chinese 2	1		2			4		5		6		
Hirajoshi 2	1				3	4				6		7
Kumoi	1		2	♭3				5		6		
Pentatonic Major	1		2		3			5		6		

6 Tone Scales

Major Blues Scale	1		2	♭3	3			5		6		
Prometheus	1		2		3		♭5			6	♭7	
Prometheus Neopolitan	1	♭2			3		♭5			6	♭7	
Six Tone Symmetrical	1	♭2			3	4			♯5	6		

7 Tone Scales

Dorian	I		2	♭3		4		5		6	♭7	
Dorian ♯4	I		2	♭3			♯4	5		6	♭7	
Hawaiian	I		2	♭3		4		5		6		7
Hungarian Major	I			♯2	3		♯4	5		6	♭7	
Ionian ♯5	I		2		3	4			♯5	6		7
Javanese	I	♭2		♭3		4		5		6	♭7	
Locrian 6	I	♭2		♭3		4	♭5			6	♭7	
Ultra Locrian	I	♭2		♭3	3		♭5		♭6	6		
Lydian	I		2		3		♯4	5		6		7
Lydian Augmented	I		2		3		♯4		♯5	6		7
Lydian Diminished	I		2	♭3			♯4	5		6		7
Lydian ♯2	I			♯2	3		♯4	5		6		7
Major (Ionian)	I		2		3	4		5		6		7
Melodic Minor (ascending)	I		2	♭3		4		5		6		7
Mixolydian	I		2		3	4		5		6	♭7	
Mohammedan	I			♭3	3	4		5	♭6	6		7
Neopolitan Major	I	♭2		♭3		4		5		6		7
Oriental (b)	I	♭2			3	4	♭5			6	♭7	
Overtone Dominant	I		2		3		♯4	5		6	♭7	
Roumanian Minor	I		2	♭3			♯4	5		6	♭7	

8 Tone Scales

Arabian (a)	I		2	♭3		4	♯4		♯5	6		7
Auxiliary Diminished Blues	I	♭2		♭3	3		♭5	5		6	♭7	
Bebop Major	I		2		3	4		5	♯5	6		7
Bebop Minor	I		2	♭3	3	4		5		6	♭7	
Bebop Dominant	I		2		3	4		5		6	♭7	7
Diminished	I		2	♭3		4	♭5		♭6	6		7
Japanese (Ichikosucho)	I		2		3	4	♯4	5		6		7
Jewish (Adonai Malakh)	I	♭2	2	♭3		4		5		6	♭7	
Octatonic (H-W)	I	♭2		♭3	3		♭5	5		6	♭7	
Octatonic (W-H)	I		2	♭3		4	♭5		♭6	6		7

9 Tone Scales

Blues Variation 3	I			♭3	3	4	♭5	5		6	♭7	7
Japanese (Taishikcho)	I		2		3	4	♯4	5		6	♯6	7
Nine Tone Scale	I		2	♯2	3		♯4	5	♯5	6		7

m7

5 Tone Scales

Dominant Pentatonic	1		2		3			5			♭7	
Iwato	1	♭2				4	♭5				♭7	
Japanese (in sen)	1	♭2				4		5			♭7	
Pelog 2	1	♭2		♭3				5			♭7	
Pentatonic Neutral	1		2			4		5			♭7	
Pentatonic Minor	1			♭3		4		5			♭7	

6 Tone Scales

Auxiliary Augmented	1		2		3		♯4		♯5		♯6	
Blues	1			♭3		4	♯4	5			♭7	
Prometheus	1		2		3		♭5			6	♭7	
Prometheus Neopolitan	1	♭2			3		♭5			6	♭7	
Whole Tone	1		2		3		♯4		♯5		♭7	

7 Tone Scales

Aeolian	1		2	♭3		4		5	♭6		♭7	
Altered	1	♭2		♭3	♭4		♭5		♭6		♭7	
Arabian (b)	1		2		3	4	♯4		♯5		♭7	
Blues Variation 1	1			♭3		4	♭5	5			♭7	7
Diminished Whole Tone	1	♭2		♭3	3		♭5		♭6		♭7	
Dorian	1		2	♭3		4		5		6	♭7	
Dorian ♯4	1		2	♭3			♯4	5		6	♭7	
Enigmatic	1	♭2			3		♯4		♯5		♯6	7
Half Diminished ♯2	1		2	♭3		4	♭5		♭6		♭7	
Hindu	1		2		3	4		5	♭6		♭7	
Hungarian Major	1			♯2	3		♯4	5		6	♭7	
Javanese	1	♭2		♭3		4		5		6	♭7	
Leading Whole Tone	1		2		3		♯4		♯5		♯6	7
Locrian	1	♭2		♭3		4	♭5		♭6		♭7	
Locrian 6	1	♭2		♭3		4	♭5			6	♭7	
Major Locrian	1		2		3	4	♭5		♭6		♭7	
Super Locrian	1	♭2		♯2	3		♯4		♯5		♭7	
Lydian Minor	1		2		3		♯4	5	♭6		♭7	
Melodic Minor (descending)	1		2	♭3		4		5	♭6		♭7	
Mixolydian	1		2		3	4		5		6	♭7	

Mixo-Blues	1			♭3	3	4	♭5	5			♭7	
Neopolitan Minor	1	♭2		♭3		4		5	♭6		♭7	
Oriental (a)	1	♭2			3	4	♭5		♭6		♭7	
Oriental (b)	1	♭2			3	4	♭5			6	♭7	
Overtone Dominant	1		2		3		♯4	5		6	♭7	
Phrygian	1	♭2		♭3		4		5	♭6		♭7	
Phrygian Major	1	♭2			3	4		5	♭6		♭7	
Roumanian Minor	1		2	♭3			♯4	5		6	♭7	
Spanish Gypsy	1	♭2			3	4		5	♭6		♭7	

8 Tone Scales

Auxiliary Diminished Blues	1	♭2		♭3	3		♭5	5		6	♭7	
Bebop Minor	1		2	♭3	3	4		5		6	♭7	
Bebop Dominant	1		2		3	4		5		6	♭7	7
Blues Variation 2	1			♭3	3	4	♭5	5			♭7	7
Eight Tone Spanish	1	♭2		♯2	3	4	♭5		♭6		♭7	
Jewish (Adonai Malakh)	1	♭2	2	♭3		4		5		6	♭7	
Jewish (Magen Abot)	1	♭2		♯2	3		♯4		♯5		♯6	7
Octatonic (H-W)	1	♭2		♭3	3		♭5	5		6	♭7	

9 Tone Scales

Blues Variation 3	1			♭3	3	4	♭5	5		6	♭7	7
Japanese (Taishikcho)	1		2		3	4	♯4	5		6	♯6	7
Moorish Phrygian	1	♭2		♭3	3	4		5	♯5		♭7	7

M7

5 Tone Scales

Chinese	1				3		♯4	5				7
Hirajoshi 2	1				3	4				6		7

6 Tone Scales

Augmented	1			♯2	3		♯4		♯5			7

7 Tone Scales

Blues Variation 1	1			♭3		4	♭5	5			♭7	7
Byzantine	1	♭2			3	4		5	♭6			7
Double Harmonic	1	♭2			3	4		5	♭6			7
Enigmatic	1	♭2			3		♯4		♯5		♯6	7
Harmonic Minor	1		2	♭3		4		5	♭6			7
Hawaiian	1		2	♭3		4		5		6		7
Hungarian Minor	1		2	♭3			♯4	5	♭6			7
Hungarian Gypsy Persian	1	♭2			3	4		5	♭6			7
Ionian ♯5	1		2		3	4			♯5	6		7
Leading Whole Tone	1		2		3		♯4		♯5		♯6	7
Lydian	1		2		3		♯4	5		6		7
Lydian Augmented	1		2		3		♯4		♯5	6		7
Lydian Diminished	1		2	♭3			♯4	5		6		7
Lydian ♯2	1			♯2	3		♯4	5		6		7
Major (Ionian)	1		2		3	4		5		6		7
Melodic Minor (ascending)	1		2	♭3		4		5		6		7
Mohammedan	1			♭3	3	4		5	♭6	6		7
Neopolitan	1	♭2		♭3		4		5	♭6			7
Neopolitan Major	1	♭2		♭3		4		5		6		7
Persian	1	♭2			3	4	♭5		♭6			7

8 Tone Scales

Algerian	1		2	♭3	3	4	♯4		♭6			7
Arabian (a)	1		2	♭3		4	♯4		♯5	6		7
Bebop Major	1		2		3	4		5	♯5	6		7
Bebop Dominant	1		2		3	4		5		6	♭7	7
Bebop Half-Diminished	1	♭2		♭3		4	♭5	5	♭6			7
Blues Variation 2	1			♭3	3	4	♭5	5			♭7	7
Diminished	1		2	♭3		4	♭5		♭6	6		7
Japanese (Ichikosucho)	1		2		3	4	♯4	5		6		7
Jewish (Magen Abot)	1	♭2		♯2	3		♯4		♯5		♯6	7
Octatonic (W-H)	1		2	♭3		4	♭5		♭6	6		7

9 Tone Scales

Blues Variation 3	1			♭3	3	4	♭5	5		6	♭7	7
Japanese (Taishikcho)	1		2		3	4	♯4	5		6	♯6	7
Moorish Phrygian	1	♭2		♭3	3	4		5	♯5		♭7	7
Nine Tone Scale	1		2	♯2	3		♯4	5	♯5	6		7

Chords

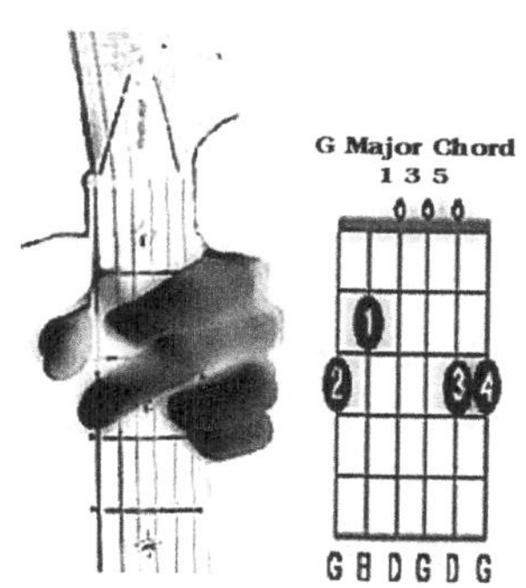

Augmented	1 3 #5
Diminished	1 ♭3 ♭5
Diminished 7th	1♭3 ♭5 6 ♭♭7
Dominant 7th	1 3 5 ♭7
Dominant 7th	1 4 5 ♭7
Dominant ♭5	1 3 ♭5 ♭7
Dominant #5	1 3 #5 ♭7
Dominant 9th	1 3 5 ♭7 9
Dominant 7th ♭9	1 3 5 ♭7 ♭9
Dominant 7th #9	1 3 5 ♭7 #9
Dominant 7th ♭5 ♭9	1 3 ♭5 ♭7 ♭9
Dominant 7th ♭ #9	1 3 5 ♭7 #9
Dominant 7th #5 ♭9	1 3 #5 ♭7 ♭9
Dominant 7th #5 #9	1 3 #5 ♭7 #9
Dominant 11th	1 3 5 ♭7 9 11
Dominant 13th	1 3 5 ♭7 9 11 13
Major	1 3 5
Major diminished 5th	1 3 ♭5
Major 6th	1 3 5 6
Major add 9	1 3 5 9
Major 7th	1 3 5 7

Major 7th ♭ 5	1 3 ♭5 7
Major 7th ♯5	1 3 ♯5 7
Major 6th add 9	1 3 5 6 9
Major 9th	1 3 5 7 9
Major 11th	1 3 5 7 9 11
Major 9th ♯11	1 3 5 7 9 ♯11
Major 13th	1 3 5 7 9 11 13
Major 13th ♯11	1 3 5 7 9 ♯11 13
Minor	1 ♭3 5
Minor 7th	1 ♭3 5 ♭7
Minor 6th	1 ♭3 5 6
Minor Major 7th	1 ♭ 3 5 7
Minor 7th ♭5	1 ♭3 ♭5 ♭7
Minor 7th♯5	1 ♭3 ♯5 ♭7
Minor 9th	1 ♭3 5 ♭7 9
Minor Major 9th	1 ♭3 5 7 9
Minor 11th	1 ♭3 5 ♭7 9 11
Minor 13th	1 ♭3 5 ♭7 9 11 13
Suspended 2nd Suspended 4th	1 2 4 5
Suspended 2nd	1 2 5
Suspended 4th	1 4 5
9 ♭5	1 3 ♭5 7 9
9 ♯5	1 3 ♯5 ♭7 9
11 ♭9	1 5 ♭7 ♭9 11
13 ♭9	1 3 5 ♭7 ♭9 13
13 ♯11	1 3 5 ♭7 9 ♯11 13

Chords

Scale-Sets

Augmented

1 3 #5

6 Tone Scales

Augmented	1			#2	3		#4		#5			7
Auxiliary Augmented	1		2		3		#4		#5		#6	
Six Tone Symmetrical	1	b2			3	4			#5	6		
Whole Tone	1		2		3		#4		#5		b7	

7 Tone Scales

Altered	1	b2		b3	b4		b5		b6		b7	
Arabian (b)	1		2		3	4	#4		#5		b7	
Byzantine	1	b2			3	4		5	b6			7
Diminished Whole Tone	1	b2		b3	3		b5		b6		b7	
Double Harmonic	1	b2			3	4		5	b6			7
Enigmatic	1	b2			3		#4		#5		#6	7
Hindu	1		2		3	4		5	b6		b7	
Hungarian Gypsy Persian	1	b2			3	4		5	b6			7
Ionian #5	1		2		3	4			#5	6		7
Leading Whole Tone	1		2		3		#4		#5		#6	7
Major Locrian	1		2		3	4	b5		b6		b7	
Super Locrian	1	b2		#2	3		#4		#5		b7	
Ultra Locrian	1	b2		b3	3		b5		b6	6		
Lydian Minor	1		2		3		#4	5	b6		b7	
Lydian Augmented	1		2		3		#4		#5	6		7
Mohammedan	1			b3	3	4		5	b6	6		7
Oriental (a)	1	b2			3	4	b5		b6		b7	
Persian	1	b2			3	4	b5		b6			7
Phrygian Major	1	b2			3	4		5	b6		b7	
Spanish Gypsy	1	b2			3	4		5	b6		b7	

8 Tone Scales

Algerian	1		2	♭3	3	4	♯4		♭6			7
Bebop Major	1		2		3	4		5	♯5	6		7
Eight Tone Spanish	1	♭2		♯2	3	4	♭5		♭6		♭7	
Jewish (Magen Abot)	1	♭2		♯2	3		♯4		♯5		♯6	7

9 Tone Scales

Moorish Phrygian	1	♭2		♭3	3	4		5	♯5		♭7	7
Nine Tone Scale	1		2	♯2	3		♯4	5	♯5	6		7

Diminished

1 ♭3 ♭5

6 Tone Scales

Augmented	1			♯2	3		♯4		♯5			7
Blues	1			♭3		4	♯4	5			♭7	

7 Tone Scales

	1	♭2	2	♭3	3	4	♭5	5	♭6	6	♭7	7
Altered	1	♭2		♭3	♭4		♭5		♭6		♭7	
Blues Variation 1	1			♭3		4	♭5	5			♭7	7
Diminished Whole Tone	1	♭2		♭3	3		♭5		♭6		♭7	
Dorian ♯4	1		2	♭3			♯4	5		6	♭7	
Half Diminished ♯2	1		2	♭3		4	♭5		♭6		♭7	
Hungarian Major	1			♯2	3		♯4	5		6	♭7	
Hungarian Minor	1		2	♭3			♯4	5	♭6			7
Locrian	1	♭2		♭3		4	♭5		♭6		♭7	
Locrian 6	1	♭2		♭3		4	♭5			6	♭7	
Lydian Diminished	1		2	♭3			♯4	5		6		7
Lydian ♯2	1			♯2	3		♯4	5		6		7
Mixo-Blues	1			♭3	3	4	♭5	5			♭7	
Roumanian Minor	1		2	♭3			♯4	5		6	♭7	

8 Tone Scales

Algerian	1		2	♭3	3	4	♯4		♭6			7
Arabian (a)	1		2	♭3		4	♯4		♯5	6		7
Auxiliary Diminished Blues	1	♭2		♭3	3		♭5	5		6	♭7	

Scale												
Bebop Half-Diminished	1	♭2		♭3		4	♭5	5	♭6			7
Blues Variation 2	1			♭3	3	4	♭5	5			♭7	7
Diminished	1		2	♭3		4	♭5		♭6	6		7
Eight Tone Spanish	1	♭2		♯2	3	4	♭5		♭6		♭7	
Jewish (Magen Abot)	1	♭2		♯2	3		♯4		♯5		♯6	7
Octatonic (H-W)	1	♭2		♭3	3		♭5	5		6	♭7	
Octatonic (W-H)	1		2	♭3		4	♭5		♭6	6		7

9 Tone Scales

Scale												
Blues Variation 3	1			♭3	3	4	♭5	5		6	♭7	7
Nine Tone Scale	1		2	♯2	3		♯4	5	♯5	6		7

Diminished 7th

1 ♭3 ♭5 6 ♭♭7

7 Tone Scales

Scale												
Dorian ♯4	1		2	♭3			♯4	5		6	♭7	
Hungarian Major	1			♯2	3		♯4	5		6	♭7	
Locrian 6	1	♭2		♭3		4	♭5			6	♭7	
Ultra Locrian	1	♭2		♭3	3		♭5		♭6	6		
Lydian Diminished	1		2	♭3			♯4	5		6		7
Lydian ♯2	1			♯2	3		♯4	5		6		7
Roumanian Minor	1		2	♭3			♯4	5		6	♭7	

8 Tone Scales

Scale												
Arabian (a)	1		2	♭3		4	♯4		♯5	6		7
Auxiliary Diminished Blues	1	♭2		♭3	3		♭5	5		6	♭7	
Diminished	1		2	♭3		4	♭5		♭6	6		7
Octatonic (H-W)	1	♭2		♭3	3		♭5	5		6	♭7	
Octatonic (W-H)	1		2	♭3		4	♭5		♭6	6		7

9 Tone Scales

Scale												
Blues Variation 3	1			♭3	3	4	♭5	5		6	♭7	7
Nine Tone Scale	1		2	♯2	3		♯4	5	♯5	6		7

Dominant 7th

1 3 5 ♭7

5 Tone Scales												
Dominant Pentatonic	1		2		3			5			♭7	

6 Tone Scales												
Blues	1			♭3		4	♯4	5			♭7	

7 Tone Scales												
Hindu	1		2		3	4		5	♭6		♭7	
Hungarian Major	1			♯2	3		♯4	5		6	♭7	
Lydian Minor	1		2		3		♯4	5	♭6		♭7	
Mixolydian	1		2		3	4		5		6	♭7	
Mixo-Blues	1			♭3	3	4	♭5	5			♭7	
Overtone Dominant	1		2		3		♯4	5		6	♭7	
Phrygian Major	1	♭2			3	4		5	♭6		♭7	
Spanish Gypsy	1	♭2			3	4		5	♭6		♭7	

8 Tone Scales												
Auxiliary Diminished Blues	1	♭2		♭3	3		♭5	5		6	♭7	
Bebop Minor	1		2	♭3	3	4		5		6	♭7	
Bebop Dominant	1		2		3	4		5		6	♭7	7
Blues Variation 2	1			♭3	3	4	♭5	5			♭7	7
Octatonic (H-W)	1	♭2		♭3	3		♭5	5		6	♭7	

9 Tone Scales												
Blues Variation 3	1			♭3	3	4	♭5	5		6	♭7	7
Japanese (Taishikcho)	1		2		3	4	♯4	5		6	♯6	7
Moorish Phrygian	1	♭2		♭3	3	4		5	♯5		♭7	7

Dominant 7th

1 4 5 ♭7

5 Tone Scales

Japanese (in sen)	1	♭2				4		5			♭7	
Pentatonic Neutral	1		2			4		5			♭7	
Pentatonic Minor	1			♭3		4		5			♭7	

6 Tone Scales

Blues	1			♭3		4	♯4	5			♭7	

7 Tone Scales

Aeolian	1		2	♭3		4		5	♭6		♭7	
Blues Variation 1	1			♭3		4	♭5	5			♭7	7
Dorian	1		2	♭3		4		5		6	♭7	
Hindu	1		2		3	4		5	♭6		♭7	
Javanese	1	♭2		♭3		4		5		6	♭7	
Melodic Minor (descending)	1		2	♭3		4		5	♭6		♭7	
Mixolydian	1		2		3	4		5		6	♭7	
Mixo-Blues	1			♭3	3	4	♭5	5			♭7	
Neopolitan Minor	1	♭2		♭3		4		5	♭6		♭7	
Phrygian	1	♭2		♭3		4		5	♭6		♭7	
Phrygian Major	1	♭2			3	4		5	♭6		♭7	
Spanish Gypsy	1	♭2			3	4		5	♭6		♭7	

8 Tone Scales

Bebop Minor	1		2	♭3	3	4		5		6	♭7	
Bebop Dominant	1		2		3	4		5		6	♭7	7
Blues Variation 2	1			♭3	3	4	♭5	5			♭7	7
Jewish (Adonai Malakh)	1	♭2	2	♭3		4		5		6	♭7	

9 Tone Scales

Blues Variation 3	1			♭3	3	4	♭5	5		6	♭7	7
Japanese (Taishikcho)	1		2		3	4	♯4	5		6	♯6	7
Moorish Phrygian	1	♭2		♭3	3	4		5	♯5		♭7	7

Dominant ♭5

1 3 ♭5 ♭7

6 Tone Scales												
Auxiliary Augmented	1		2		3		♯4		♯5		♯6	
Prometheus	1		2		3		♭5			6	♭7	
Prometheus Neopolitan	1	♭2			3		♭5			6	♭7	
Whole Tone	1		2		3		♯4		♯5		♭7	

7 Tone Scales												
Arabian (b)	1		2		3	4	♯4		♯5		♭7	
Diminished Whole Tone	1	♭2		♭3	3		♭5		♭6		♭7	
Enigmatic	1	♭2			3		♯4		♯5		♯6	7
Hungarian Major	1			♯2	3		♯4	5		6	♭7	
Leading Whole Tone	1		2		3		♯4		♯5		♯6	7
Major Locrian	1		2		3	4	♭5		♭6		♭7	
Super Locrian	1	♭2		♯2	3		♯4		♯5		♭7	
Lydian Minor	1		2		3		♯4	5	♭6		♭7	
Mixo-Blues	1			♭3	3	4	♭5	5			♭7	
Oriental (a)	1	♭2			3	4	♭5		♭6		♭7	
Oriental (b)	1	♭2			3	4	♭5			6	♭7	
Overtone Dominant	1		2		3		♯4	5		6	♭7	

8 Tone Scales												
Auxiliary Diminished Blues	1	♭2		♭3	3		♭5	5		6	♭7	
Blues Variation 2	1			♭3	3	4	♭5	5			♭7	7
Eight Tone Spanish	1	♭2		♯2	3	4	♭5		♭6		♭7	
Jewish (Magen Abot)	1	♭2		♯2	3		♯4		♯5		♯6	7
Octatonic (H-W)	1	♭2		♭3	3		♭5	5		6	♭7	

9 Tone Scales												
Blues Variation 3	1			♭3	3	4	♭5	5		6	♭7	7
Japanese (Taishikcho)	1		2		3	4	♯4	5		6	♯6	7

Dominant ♯5

1 3 ♯5 ♭7

6 Tone Scales

Auxiliary Augmented	1		2		3		♯4		♯5	♯6	
Whole Tone	1		2		3		♯4		♯5	♭7	

7 Tone Scales

Arabian (b)	1		2		3	4	♯4		♯5	♭7	
Diminished Whole Tone	1	♭2		♭3	3		♭5		♭6	♭7	
Enigmatic	1	♭2			3		♯4		♯5	♯6	7
Hindu	1		2		3	4		5	♭6	♭7	
Leading Whole Tone	1		2		3		♯4		♯5	♯6	7
Major Locrian	1		2		3	4	♭5		♭6	♭7	
Super Locrian	1	♭2		♯2	3		♯4		♯5	♭7	
Lydian Minor	1		2		3		♯4	5	♭6	♭7	
Oriental (a)	1	♭2			3	4	♭5		♭6	♭7	
Phrygian Major	1	♭2			3	4		5	♭6	♭7	
Spanish Gypsy	1	♭2			3	4		5	♭6	♭7	

8 Tone Scales

Eight Tone Spanish	1	♭2		♯2	3	4	♭5		♭6	♭7	
Jewish (Magen Abot)	1	♭2		♯2	3		♯4		♯5	♯6	7

9 Tone Scales

Moorish Phrygian	1	♭2		♭3	3	4		5	♯5	♭7	7

Dominant 9th

1 3 5 ♭7 9

5 Tone Scales

Dominant Pentatonic	1		2		3			5		♭7	

7 Tone Scales

Hindu	1		2		3	4		5	b6		b7	
Lydian Minor	1		2		3		#4	5	b6		b7	
Mixolydian	1		2		3	4		5		6	b7	
Overtone Dominant	1		2		3		#4	5		6	b7	

8 Tone Scales

Bebop Minor	1		2	b3	3	4		5		6	b7	
Bebop Dominant	1		2		3	4		5		6	b7	7

9 Tone Scales

Japanese (Taishikcho)	1		2		3	4	#4	5		6	#6	7

Dominant 7th b9

1 3 5 b7 b9

7 Tone Scales

Phrygian Major	1	b2			3	4		5	b6		b7	
Spanish Gypsy	1	b2			3	4		5	b6		b7	

8 Tone Scales

Auxiliary Diminished Blues	1	b2		b3	3		b5	5		6	b7	
Octatonic (H-W)	1	b2		b3	3		b5	5		6	b7	

9 Tone Scales

Moorish Phrygian	1	b2		b3	3	4		5	#5		b7	7

Dominant 7th #9

1 3 5 b7 #9

7 Tone Scales

Hungarian Major	1			#2	3		#4	5		6	b7	

Mixo-Blues	1			♭3	3	4	♭5	5			♭7	

8 Tone Scales

Auxiliary Diminished Blues	1	♭2		♭3	3		♭5	5		6	♭7	
Bebop Minor	1		2	♭3	3	4		5		6	♭7	
Blues Variation 2	1			♭3	3	4	♭5	5			♭7	7
Octatonic (H-W)	1	♭2		♭3	3		♭5	5		6	♭7	

9 Tone Scales

Blues Variation 3	1			♭3	3	4	♭5	5		6	♭7	7
Moorish Phrygian	1	♭2		♭3	3	4		5	♯5		♭7	7

Dominant 7th ♭5 ♭9

1 3 ♭5 ♭7 ♭9

6 Tone Scales

Prometheus Neopolitan	1	♭2			3		♭5			6	♭7	

7 Tone Scales

Altered	1	♭2		♭3	♭4		♭5		♭6		♭7	
Diminished Whole Tone	1	♭2		♭3	3		♭5		♭6		♭7	
Enigmatic	1	♭2			3		♯4		♯5	♯6		7
Super Locrian	1	♭2		♯2	3		♯4		♯5		♭7	
Oriental (a)	1	♭2			3	4	♭5		♭6		♭7	
Oriental (b)	1	♭2			3	4	♭5			6	♭7	

8 Tone Scales

Auxiliary Diminished Blues	1	♭2		♭3	3		♭5	5		6	♭7	
Eight Tone Spanish	1	♭2		♯2	3	4	♭5		♭6		♭7	
Jewish (Magen Abot)	1	♭2		♯2	3		♯4		♯5	♯6		7
Octatonic (H-W)	1	♭2		♭3	3		♭5	5		6	♭7	

Dominant 7th ♭ ♯9

1 3 5 ♭7 ♯9

7 Tone Scales

Hungarian Major	1			♯2	3		♯4	5		6	♭7	
Super Locrian	1	♭2		♯2	3		♯4		♯5		♭7	
Mixolydian	1		2		3	4		5		6	♭7	
Mixo-Blues	1			♭3	3	4	♭5	5			♭7	

8 Tone Scales

Auxiliary Diminished Blues	1	♭2		♭3	3		♭5	5		6	♭7	
Bebop Minor	1		2	♭3	3	4		5		6	♭7	
Blues Variation 2	1			♭3	3	4	♭5	5			♭7	7
Octatonic (H-W)	1	♭2		♭3	3		♭5	5		6	♭7	

9 Tone Scales

Blues Variation 3	1			♭3	3	4	♭5	5		6	♭7	7
Moorish Phrygian	1	♭2		♭3	3	4		5	♯5		♭7	7

Dominant 7th ♯5 ♭9

1 3 ♯5 ♭7 ♭9

7 Tone Scales

Altered	1	♭2	♭3	♭4		♭5		♭6		♭7	
Diminished Whole Tone	1	♭2	♭3	3		♭5		♭6		♭7	
Enigmatic	1	♭2		3		♯4		♯5		♯6	7
Super Locrian	1	♭2	♯2	3		♯4		♯5		♭7	
Oriental (a)	1	♭2		3	4	♭5		♭6		♭7	
Phrygian Major	1	♭2		3	4		5	♭6		♭7	
Spanish Gypsy	1	♭2		3	4		5	♭6		♭7	

8 Tone Scales

Eight Tone Spanish	1	♭2	♯2	3	4	♭5		♭6		♭7	
Jewish (Magen Abot)	1	♭2	♯2	3		♯4		♯5		♯6	7

9 Tone Scales

Moorish Phrygian	1	b2	b3	3	4		5	#5		b7	7

Dominant 7th #5 #9

1 3 #5 b7 #9

7 Tone Scales

Diminished Whole Tone	1	b2	b3	3	b5	b6	b7	
Super Locrian	1	b2	#2	3	#4	#5	b7	

8 Tone Scales

Eight Tone Spanish	1	b2	#2	3	4	b5	b6	b7	
Jewish (Magen Abot)	1	b2	#2	3		#4	#5	#6	7

9 Tone Scales

Moorish Phrygian	1	b2	b3	3	4	5	#5	b7	7

Dominant 11th

1 3 5 b7 9 11

7 Tone Scales

Hindu	1	2	3	4	5	b6		b7
Mixolydian	1	2	3	4	5		6	b7

8 Tone Scales

Bebop Minor	1	2	b3	3	4	5	6	b7	
Bebop Dominant	1	2		3	4	5	6	b7	7

9 Tone Scales

Japanese (Taishikcho)	1	2	3	4	#4	5	6	#6	7

Dominant 13th

1 3 5 ♭7 9 11 13

7 Tone Scales

Scale												
Mixolydian	1		2		3	4		5		6	♭7	

8 Tone Scales

Scale												
Bebop Minor	1		2	♭3	3	4		5		6	♭7	
Bebop Dominant	1		2		3	4		5		6	♭7	7

9 Tone Scales

Scale												
Japanese (Taishikcho)	1		2		3	4	♯4	5		6	♯6	7

Major

1 3 5

5 Tone Scales

Scale												
Chinese	1				3		♯4	5				7
Dominant Pentatonic	1		2		3			5			♭7	
Pentatonic Major	1		2		3			5		6		

6 Tone Scales

Scale												
Major Blues Scale	1		2	♭3	3			5		6		

7 Tone Scales

Scale												
Byzantine	1	♭2			3	4		5	♭6			7
Double Harmonic	1	♭2			3	4		5	♭6			7
Hindu	1		2		3	4		5	♭6		♭7	
Hungarian Major	1			♯2	3		♯4	5		6	♭7	
Hungarian Gypsy Persian	1	♭2			3	4		5	♭6			7
Lydian	1		2		3		♯4	5		6		7
Lydian Minor	1		2		3		♯4	5	♭6		♭7	
Lydian ♯2	1			♯2	3		♯4	5		6		7

Major (Ionian)	1		2		3	4		5		6		7
Mixolydian	1		2		3	4		5		6	b7	
Mixo-Blues	1			b3	3	4	b5	5			b7	
Mohammedan	1			b3	3	4		5	b6	6		7
Overtone Dominant	1		2		3		#4	5		6	b7	
Phrygian Major	1	b2			3	4		5	b6		b7	
Spanish Gypsy	1	b2			3	4		5	b6		b7	

8 Tone Scales

Auxiliary Diminished Blues	1	b2		b3	3		b5	5		6	b7	
Bebop Major	1		2		3	4		5	#5	6		7
Bebop Minor	1		2	b3	3	4		5		6	b7	
Bebop Dominant	1		2		3	4		5		6	b7	7
Blues Variation 2	1			b3	3	4	b5	5			b7	7
Japanese (Ichikosucho)	1		2		3	4	#4	5		6		7
Octatonic (H-W)	1	b2		b3	3		b5	5		6	b7	

9 Tone Scales

Blues Variation 3	1			b3	3	4	b5	5		6	b7	7
Japanese (Taishikcho)	1		2		3	4	#4	5		6	#6	7
Moorish Phrygian	1	b2		b3	3	4		5	#5		b7	7
Nine Tone Scale	1		2	#2	3		#4	5	#5	6		7

Major diminished 5th

1 3 b5

5 Tone Scales

Chinese	1				3		#4	5				7

6 Tone Scales

Augmented	1			#2	3		#4		#5			7
Auxiliary Augmented	1		2		3		#4		#5		#6	
Prometheus	1		2		3		b5			6	b7	
Prometheus Neopolitan	1	b2			3		b5			6	b7	
Whole Tone	1		2		3		#4		#5		b7	

7 Tone Scales

Arabian (b)	1		2		3	4	♯4		♯5		♭7	
Diminished Whole Tone	1	♭2		♭3	3		♭5		♭6		♭7	
Enigmatic	1	♭2			3		♯4		♯5		♯6	7
Hungarian Major	1			♯2	3		♯4	5		6	♭7	
Leading Whole Tone	1		2		3		♯4		♯5		♯6	7
Major Locrian	1		2		3	4	♭5		♭6		♭7	
Super Locrian	1	♭2		♯2	3		♯4		♯5		♭7	
Ultra Locrian	1	♭2		♭3	3		♭5		♭6	6		
Lydian	1		2		3		♯4	5		6		7
Lydian Minor	1		2		3		♯4	5	♭6		♭7	
Lydian Augmented	1		2		3		♯4		♯5	6		7
Lydian Diminished	1		2	♭3			♯4	5		6		7
Lydian ♯2	1			♯2	3		♯4	5		6		7
Mixo-Blues	1			♭3	3	4	♭5	5			♭7	
Oriental (a)	1	♭2			3	4	♭5		♭6		♭7	
Oriental (b)	1	♭2			3	4	♭5			6	♭7	
Overtone Dominant	1		2		3		♯4	5		6	♭7	
Persian	1	♭2			3	4	♭5		♭6			7

8 Tone Scales

Algerian	1		2	♭3	3	4	♯4		♭6			7
Auxiliary Diminished Blues	1	♭2		♭3	3		♭5	5		6	♭7	
Blues Variation 2	1			♭3	3	4	♭5	5			♭7	7
Eight Tone Spanish	1	♭2		♯2	3	4	♭5		♭6		♭7	
Japanese (Ichikosucho)	1		2		3	4	♯4	5		6		7
Jewish (Magen Abot)	1	♭2		♯2	3		♯4		♯5		♯6	7
Octatonic (H-W)	1	♭2		♭3	3		♭5	5		6	♭7	

9 Tone Scales

Blues Variation 3	1			♭3	3	4	♭5	5		6	♭7	7
Japanese (Taishikcho)	1		2		3	4	♯4	5		6	♯6	7
Nine Tone Scale	1		2	♯2	3		♯4	5	♯5	6		7

Major 6th

1 3 5 6

5 Tone Scales

Pentatonic Major	1		2		3			5		6		

6 Tone Scales

Major Blues Scale	1		2	♭3	3			5		6		

7 Tone Scales

Hungarian Major	1			♯2	3		♯4	5		6	♭7	
Lydian	1		2		3		♯4	5		6		7
Lydian ♯2	1			♯2	3		♯4	5		6		7
Major (Ionian)	1		2		3	4		5		6		7
Mixolydian	1		2		3	4		5		6	♭7	
Mohammedan	1			♭3	3	4		5	♭6	6		7
Overtone Dominant	1		2		3		♯4	5		6	♭7	
Spanish Gypsy	1	♭2			3	4		5	♭6		♭7	

8 Tone Scales

Auxiliary Diminished Blues	1	♭2		♭3	3		♭5	5		6	♭7	
Bebop Major	1		2		3	4		5	♯5	6		7
Bebop Minor	1		2	♭3	3	4		5		6	♭7	
Bebop Dominant	1		2		3	4		5		6	♭7	7
Japanese (Ichikosucho)	1		2		3	4	♯4	5		6		7
Octatonic (H-W)	1	♭2		♭3	3		♭5	5		6	♭7	

9 Tone Scales

Blues Variation 3	1			♭3	3	4	♭5	5		6	♭7	7
Japanese (Taishikcho)	1		2		3	4	♯4	5		6	♯6	7
Nine Tone Scale	1		2	♯2	3		♯4	5	♯5	6		7

Major add 9
1 3 5 9

5 Tone Scales

Dominant Pentatonic	1	2		3			5			♭7	
Pentatonic Major	1	2		3			5		6		

6 Tone Scales

Major Blues Scale	1	2	♭3	3			5		6		

7 Tone Scales

Hindu	1	2		3	4		5	♭6		♭7	
Lydian	1	2		3		♯4	5		6		7
Lydian Minor	1	2		3		♯4	5	♭6		♭7	
Major (Ionian)	1	2		3	4		5		6		7
Mixolydian	1	2		3	4		5		6	♭7	
Overtone Dominant	1	2		3		♯4	5		6	♭7	

8 Tone Scales

Bebop Major	1	2		3	4		5	♯5	6		7
Bebop Minor	1	2	♭3	3	4		5		6	♭7	
Bebop Dominant	1	2		3	4		5		6	♭7	7
Japanese (Ichikosucho)	1	2		3	4	♯4	5		6		7

9 Tone Scales

Japanese (Taishikcho)	1	2		3	4	♯4	5		6	♯6	7
Nine Tone Scale	1	2	♯2	3		♯4	5	♯5	6		7

Major 7th
1 3 5 7

5 Tone Scales

Chinese	1			3		♯4	5				7

7 Tone Scales

Byzantine	1	♭2			3	4		5	♭6			7
Double Harmonic	1	♭2			3	4		5	♭6			7
Hungarian Gypsy Persian	1	♭2			3	4		5	♭6			7
Lydian	1		2		3		#4	5		6		7
Lydian #2	1			#2	3		#4	5		6		7
Major (Ionian)	1		2		3	4		5		6		7
Mohammedan	1			♭3	3	4		5	♭6	6		7

8 Tone Scales

Bebop Major	1		2		3	4		5	#5	6		7
Bebop Dominant	1		2		3	4		5		6	♭7	7
Blues Variation 2	1			♭3	3	4	♭5	5			♭7	7
Japanese (Ichikosucho)	1		2		3	4	#4	5		6		7

9 Tone Scales

Blues Variation 3	1			♭3	3	4	♭5	5		6	♭7	7
Japanese (Taishikcho)	1		2		3	4	#4	5		6	#6	7
Moorish Phrygian	1	♭2		♭3	3	4		5	#5		♭7	7
Nine Tone Scale	1		2	#2	3		#4	5	#5	6		7

Major 7th ♭ 5

1 3 ♭5 7

5 Tone Scales

Chinese	1				3		#4	5				7

6 Tone Scales

Augmented	1			#2	3		#4		#5			7

7 Tone Scales

Enigmatic	1	♭2			3		#4		#5		#6	7
Leading Whole Tone	1		2		3		#4		#5		#6	7
Lydian	1		2		3		#4	5		6		7
Lydian Augmented	1		2		3		#4		#5	6		7

Lydian ♯2	1			♯2	3		♯4	5		6		7
Persian	1	♭2			3	4	♭5		♭6			7

8 Tone Scales

Algerian	1		2	♭3	3	4	♯4		♭6			7
Blues Variation 2	1			♭3	3	4	♭5	5			♭7	7
Japanese (Ichikosucho)	1		2		3	4	♯4	5		6		7
Jewish (Magen Abot)	1	♭2		♯2	3		♯4		♯5		♯6	7

9 Tone Scales

Blues Variation 3	1			♭3	3	4	♭5	5		6	♭7	7
Japanese (Taishikcho)	1		2		3	4	♯4	5		6	♯6	7
Moorish Phrygian	1	♭2		♭3	3	4		5	♯5		♭7	7
Nine Tone Scale	1		2	♯2	3		♯4	5	♯5	6		7

Major 7th ♯5
1 3 ♯5 7

6 Tone Scales

Augmented	1			♯2	3		♯4		♯5			7

7 Tone Scales

Byzantine	1	♭2			3	4		5	♭6			7
Double Harmonic	1	♭2			3	4		5	♭6			7
Enigmatic	1	♭2			3		♯4		♯5		♯6	7
Hungarian Gypsy Persian	1	♭2			3	4		5	♭6			7
Ionian ♯5	1		2		3	4			♯5	6		7
Leading Whole Tone	1		2		3		♯4		♯5		♯6	7
Lydian Augmented	1		2		3		♯4		♯5	6		7
Mohammedan	1			♭3	3	4		5	♭6	6		7
Persian	1	♭2			3	4	♭5		♭6			7

8 Tone Scales

Algerian	1		2	♭3	3	4	♯4		♭6			7
Bebop Major	1		2		3	4		5	♯5	6		7
Jewish (Magen Abot)	1	♭2		♯2	3		♯4		♯5		♯6	7

9 Tone Scales

Moorish Phrygian	1	b2		b3	3	4		5	#5		b7	7
Nine Tone Scale	1		2	#2	3		#4	5	#5	6		7

Major 6th add 9
1 3 5 6 9

5 Tone Scales

Pentatonic Major	1		2		3			5		6		

6 Tone Scales

Major Blues Scale	1		2	b3	3			5		6		

7 Tone Scales

Lydian	1		2		3		#4	5		6		7
Major (Ionian)	1		2		3	4		5		6		7
Mixolydian	1		2		3	4		5		6	b7	
Overtone Dominant	1		2		3		#4	5		6	b7	

8 Tone Scales

Bebop Major	1		2		3	4		5	#5	6		7
Bebop Minor	1		2	b3	3	4		5		6	b7	
Bebop Dominant	1		2		3	4		5		6	b7	7
Japanese (Ichikosucho)	1		2		3	4	#4	5		6		7

9 Tone Scales

Japanese (Taishikcho)	1		2		3	4	#4	5		6	#6	7
Nine Tone Scale	1		2	#2	3		#4	5	#5	6		7

Major 9th

1 3 5 7 9

7 Tone Scales

Lydian	1	2		3		#4	5		6		7
Major (Ionian)	1	2		3	4		5		6		7

8 Tone Scales

Bebop Major	1	2		3	4		5	#5	6		7
Bebop Dominant	1	2		3	4		5		6	b7	7
Japanese (Ichikosucho)	1	2		3	4	#4	5		6		7

9 Tone Scales

Japanese (Taishikcho)	1	2		3	4	#4	5		6	#6	7
Nine Tone Scale	1	2	#2	3		#4	5	#5	6		7

Major 11th

1 3 5 7 9 11

7 Tone Scales

Major (Ionian)	1	2		3	4		5		6		7

8 Tone Scales

Bebop Major	1	2		3	4		5	#5	6		7
Bebop Dominant	1	2		3	4		5		6	b7	7
Japanese (Ichikosucho)	1	2		3	4	#4	5		6		7

9 Tone Scales

Japanese (Taishikcho)	1	2		3	4	#4	5		6	#6	7

Major 9th #11
1 3 5 7 9 #11

7 Tone Scales											
Lydian	1	2		3		#4	5		6		7
8 Tone Scales											
Japanese (Ichikosucho)	1	2		3	4	#4	5		6		7
9 Tone Scales											
Japanese (Taishikcho)	1	2		3	4	#4	5		6	#6	7
Nine Tone Scale	1	2	#2	3		#4	5	#5	6		7

Major 13th
1 3 5 7 9 11 13

7 Tone Scales											
Major (Ionian)	1	2		3	4		5		6		7
8 Tone Scales											
Bebop Major	1	2		3	4		5	#5	6		7
Bebop Dominant	1	2		3	4		5		6	b7	7
Japanese (Ichikosucho)	1	2		3	4	#4	5		6		7
9 Tone Scales											
Japanese (Taishikcho)	1	2		3	4	#4	5		6	#6	7

Major 13th #11
1 3 5 7 9 #11 13

7 Tone Scales							
Lydian	1	2	3	#4	5	6	7

8 Tone Scales

Scale												
Japanese (Ichikosucho)	1		2		3	4	♯4	5		6		7

9 Tone Scales

Scale												
Japanese (Taishikcho)	1		2		3	4	♯4	5		6	♯6	7
Nine Tone Scale	1		2	♯2	3		♯4	5	♯5	6		7

Minor

1 ♭3 5

5 Tone Scales

Scale												
Hirajoshi	1		2	♭3				5	♭6			
Kumoi	1		2	♭3				5		6		
Pelog	1	♭2		♭3				5	♭6			
Pelog 2	1	♭2		♭3				5			♭7	
Pentatonic Minor	1			♭3		4		5			♭7	

6 Tone Scales

Scale												
Blues	1			♭3		4	♯4	5			♭7	
Major Blues Scale	1		2	♭3	3			5		6		

7 Tone Scales

Scale												
Aeolian	1		2	♭3		4		5	♭6		♭7	
Blues Variation 1	1			♭3		4	♭5	5			♭7	7
Dorian	1		2	♭3		4		5		6	♭7	
Dorian ♯4	1		2	♭3			♯4	5		6	♭7	
Harmonic Minor	1		2	♭3		4		5	♭6			7
Hawaiian	1		2	♭3		4		5		6		7
Hungarian Major	1			♯2	3		♯4	5		6	♭7	
Hungarian Minor	1		2	♭3			♯4	5	♭6			7
Javanese	1	♭2		♭3		4		5		6	♭7	
Lydian Diminished	1		2	♭3			♯4	5		6		7
Lydian ♯2	1			♯2	3		♯4	5		6		7
Melodic Minor (ascending)	1		2	♭3		4		5		6		7
Melodic Minor (descending)	1		2	♭3		4		5	♭6		♭7	
Mixo-Blues	1			♭3	3	4	♭5	5			♭7	

Mohammedan	1			♭3	3	4		5	♭6	6		7
Neopolitan	1	♭2		♭3		4		5	♭6			7
Neopolitan Major	1	♭2		♭3		4		5		6		7
Neopolitan Minor	1	♭2		♭3		4		5	♭6		♭7	
Phrygian	1	♭2		♭3		4		5	♭6		♭7	
Roumanian Minor	1		2	♭3			♯4	5		6	♭7	

8 Tone Scales

Auxiliary Diminished Blues	1	♭2		♭3	3		♭5	5		6	♭7	
Bebop Minor	1		2	♭3	3	4		5		6	♭7	
Bebop Half-Diminished	1	♭2		♭3		4	♭5	5	♭6			7
Blues Variation 2	1			♭3	3	4	♭5	5			♭7	7
Jewish (Adonai Malakh)	1	♭2	2	♭3		4		5		6	♭7	
Octatonic (H-W)	1	♭2		♭3	3		♭5	5		6	♭7	

9 Tone Scales

Blues Variation 3	1			♭3	3	4	♭5	5		6	♭7	7
Moorish Phrygian	1	♭2		♭3	3	4		5	♯5		♭7	7
Nine Tone Scale	1		2	♯2	3		♯4	5	♯5	6		7
	1	♭2	2	♭3	3	4	♭5	5	♭6	6	♭7	7

Minor 7th

1 ♭3 5 ♭7

5 Tone Scales

Pelog 2	1	♭2		♭3				5			♭7	
Pentatonic Major	1		2		3			5		6		
Pentatonic Neutral	1		2			4		5			♭7	
Pentatonic Minor	1			♭3		4		5			♭7	

6 Tone Scales

Blues	1			♭3		4	♯4	5			♭7	

7 Tone Scales

Aeolian	1		2	♭3		4		5	♭6		♭7	
Blues Variation 1	1			♭3		4	♭5	5			♭7	7

Dorian	1		2	♭3		4		5		6	♭7	
Dorian ♯4	1		2	♭3			♯4	5		6	♭7	
Hungarian Major	1			♯2	3		♯4	5		6	♭7	
Javanese	1	♭2		♭3		4		5		6	♭7	
Melodic Minor (descending)	1		2	♭3		4		5	♭6		♭7	
Mixo-Blues	1			♭3	3	4	♭5	5			♭7	
Neopolitan Minor	1	♭2		♭3		4		5	♭6		♭7	
Phrygian	1	♭2		♭3		4		5	♭6		♭7	
Roumanian Minor	1		2	♭3			♯4	5		6	♭7	

8 Tone Scales

Auxiliary Diminished Blues	1	♭2		♭3	3		♭5	5		6	♭7	
Bebop Minor	1		2	♭3	3	4		5		6	♭7	
Blues Variation 2	1			♭3	3	4	♭5	5			♭7	7
Jewish (Adonai Malakh)	1	♭2	2	♭3		4		5		6	♭7	
Octatonic (H-W)	1	♭2		♭3	3		♭5	5		6	♭7	

9 Tone Scales

Blues Variation 3	1			♭3	3	4	♭5	5		6	♭7	7
Moorish Phrygian	1	♭2		♭3	3	4		5	♯5		♭7	7

Minor 6th

1 ♭3 5 6

5 Tone Scales

Kumoi	1		2	♭3				5		6		

6 Tone Scales

	1	♭2	2	♭3	3	4	♭5	5	♭6	6	♭7	7
Major Blues Scale	1		2	♭3	3			5		6		
Prometheus Neopolitan	1	♭2			3		♭5			6	♭7	

7 Tone Scales

Dorian	1		2	♭3		4		5		6	♭7	
Dorian ♯4	1		2	♭3			♯4	5		6	♭7	
Hawaiian	1		2	♭3		4		5		6		7
Hungarian Major	1			♯2	3		♯4	5		6	♭7	

Javanese	1	♭2		♭3		4		5		6	♭7	
Lydian Diminished	1		2	♭3			♯4	5		6		7
Lydian ♯2	1			♯2	3		♯4	5		6		7
Melodic Minor (ascending)	1		2	♭3		4		5		6		7
Mohammedan	1			♭3	3	4		5	♭6	6		7
Neopolitan Major	1	♭2		♭3		4		5		6		7
Roumanian Minor	1		2	♭3			♯4	5		6	♭7	

8 Tone Scales

Auxiliary Diminished Blues	1	♭2		♭3	3		♭5	5		6	♭7	
Bebop Minor	1		2	♭3	3	4		5		6	♭7	
Jewish (Adonai Malakh)	1	♭2	2	♭3		4		5		6	♭7	
Octatonic (H-W)	1	♭2		♭3	3		♭5	5		6	♭7	

9 Tone Scales

Blues Variation 3	1			♭3	3	4	♭5	5		6	♭7	7
Nine Tone Scale	1		2	♯2	3		♯4	5	♯5	6		7

Minor Major 7th
1 ♭3 5 7

7 Tone Scales

Blues Variation 1	1			♭3		4	♭5	5			♭7	7
Harmonic Minor	1		2	♭3		4		5	♭6			7
Hawaiian	1		2	♭3		4		5		6		7
Hungarian Minor	1		2	♭3			♯4	5	♭6			7
Lydian Diminished	1		2	♭3			♯4	5		6		7
Lydian ♯2	1			♯2	3		♯4	5		6		7
Melodic Minor (ascending)	1		2	♭3		4		5		6		7
Mohammedan	1			♭3	3	4		5	♭6	6		7
Neopolitan	1	♭2		♭3		4		5	♭6			7
Neopolitan Major	1	♭2		♭3		4		5		6		7

8 Tone Scales

Bebop Half-Diminished	1	♭2		♭3		4	♭5	5	♭6			7
Blues Variation 2	1			♭3	3	4	♭5	5			♭7	7

9 Tone Scales

Blues Variation 3	1			♭3	3	4	♭5	5		6	♭7	7
Moorish Phrygian	1	♭2		♭3	3	4		5	♯5		♭7	7
Nine Tone Scale	1		2	♯2	3		♯4	5	♯5	6		7

Minor 7th ♭5

1 ♭3 ♭5 ♭7

6 Tone Scales

Blues	1			♭3		4	♯4	5			♭7	

7 Tone Scales

Altered	1	♭2		♭3	♭4		♭5		♭6		♭7	
Blues Variation 1	1			♭3		4	♭5	5			♭7	7
Diminished Whole Tone	1	♭2		♭3	3		♭5		♭6		♭7	
Dorian ♯4	1		2	♭3			♯4	5		6	♭7	
Half Diminished ♯2	1		2	♭3		4	♭5		♭6		♭7	
Hungarian Major	1			♯2	3		♯4	5		6	♭7	
Locrian	1	♭2		♭3		4	♭5		♭6		♭7	
Locrian 6	1	♭2		♭3		4	♭5			6	♭7	
Super Locrian	1	♭2		♯2	3		♯4		♯5		♭7	
Mixo-Blues	1			♭3	3	4	♭5	5			♭7	
Roumanian Minor	1		2	♭3			♯4	5		6	♭7	

8 Tone Scales

Auxiliary Diminished Blues	1	♭2		♭3	3		♭5	5		6	♭7	
Blues Variation 2	1			♭3	3	4	♭5	5			♭7	7
Eight Tone Spanish	1	♭2		♯2	3	4	♭5		♭6		♭7	
Octatonic (H-W)	1	♭2		♭3	3		♭5	5		6	♭7	

9 Tone Scales

Blues Variation 3	1			♭3	3	4	♭5	5		6	♭7	7

Minor 7th♯5

1 ♭3 ♯5 ♭7

7 Tone Scales

Altered	1	♭2		♭3	♭4		♭5		♭6		♭7	
Diminished Whole Tone	1	♭2		♭3	3		♭5		♭6		♭7	
Half Diminished ♯2	1		2	♭3		4	♭5		♭6		♭7	
Locrian	1	♭2		♭3		4	♭5		♭6		♭7	
Super Locrian	1	♭2		♯2	3		♯4		♯5		♭7	
Melodic Minor (descending)	1		2	♭3		4		5	♭6		♭7	
Neopolitan Minor	1	♭2		♭3		4		5	♭6		♭7	
Phrygian	1	♭2		♭3		4		5	♭6		♭7	

8 Tone Scales

Eight Tone Spanish	1	♭2		♯2	3	4	♭5		♭6		♭7	
Jewish (Magen Abot)	1	♭2		♯2	3		♯4		♯5		♯6	7

9 Tone Scales

Moorish Phrygian	1	♭2		♭3	3	4		5	♯5		♭7	7

Minor 9th

1 ♭3 5 ♭7 9

7 Tone Scales

Aeolian	1		2	♭3		4		5	♭6		♭7	
Dorian	1		2	♭3		4		5		6	♭7	
Dorian ♯4	1		2	♭3			♯4	5		6	♭7	
Melodic Minor (descending)	1		2	♭3		4		5	♭6		♭7	
Roumanian Minor	1		2	♭3			♯4	5		6	♭7	

8 Tone Scales

Bebop Minor	1		2	♭3	3	4		5		6	♭7	
Jewish (Adonai Malakh)	1	♭2	2	♭3		4		5		6	♭7	

Minor Major 9th

1 ♭3 5 7 9

7 Tone Scales

Harmonic Minor	1		2	♭3		4		5	♭6			7
Hawaiian	1		2	♭3		4		5		6		7
Hungarian Minor	1		2	♭3			♯4	5	♭6			7
Lydian Diminished	1		2	♭3			♯4	5		6		7
Melodic Minor (ascending)	1		2	♭3		4		5		6		7

9 Tone Scales

Nine Tone Scale	1		2	♯2	3		♯4	5	♯5	6		7

Minor 11th

1 ♭3 5 ♭7 9 11

7 Tone Scales

Aeolian	1		2	♭3		4		5	♭6		♭7	
Dorian	1		2	♭3		4		5		6	♭7	
Melodic Minor (descending)	1		2	♭3		4		5	♭6		♭7	

8 Tone Scales

Bebop Minor	1		2	♭3	3	4		5		6	♭7	
Jewish (Adonai Malakh)	1	♭2	2	♭3		4		5		6	♭7	

Minor 13th

1 ♭3 5 ♭7 9 11 13

7 Tone Scales

Dorian	1		2	♭3		4		5		6	♭7	
Melodic Minor (descending)	1		2	♭3		4		5	♭6		♭7	

8 Tone Scales

Bebop Minor	1		2	b3	3	4		5		6	b7	
Jewish (Adonai Malakh)	1	b2	2	b3		4		5		6	b7	

9 Tone Scales

Blues Variation 3	1			b3	3	4	b5	5		6	b7	7
Japanese (Taishikcho)	1		2		3	4	#4	5		6	#6	7
Moorish Phrygian	1	b2		b3	3	4		5	#5		b7	7
Nine Tone Scale	1		2	#2	3		#4	5	#5	6		7

Suspended 2nd Suspended 4th
1 2 4 5

5 Tone Scales

Chinese 2	1		2			4		5		6		
Japanese (b)	1		2			4		5	b6			
Pentatonic Neutral	1		2			4		5			b7	

7 Tone Scales

Aeolian	1		2	b3		4		5	b6		b7	
Dorian	1		2	b3		4		5		6	b7	
Harmonic Minor	1		2	b3		4		5	b6			7
Hawaiian	1		2	b3		4		5		6		7
Hindu	1		2		3	4		5	b6		b7	
Major (Ionian)	1		2		3	4		5		6		7
Melodic Minor (ascending)	1		2	b3		4		5		6		7
Melodic Minor (descending)	1		2	b3		4		5	b6		b7	
Mixolydian	1		2		3	4		5		6	b7	

8 Tone Scales

Bebop Major	1		2		3	4		5	#5	6		7
Bebop Minor	1		2	b3	3	4		5		6	b7	
Bebop Dominant	1		2		3	4		5		6	b7	7
Japanese (Ichikosucho)	1		2		3	4	#4	5		6		7
Jewish (Adonai Malakh)	1	b2	2	b3		4		5		6	b7	

9 Tone Scales

Scale									
Japanese (Taishikcho)	1	2	3	4	♯4	5	6	♯6	7

Suspended 2nd
1 2 5

5 Tone Scales

Scale								
Chinese 2	1	2			4	5		6	
Dominant Pentatonic	1	2		3		5			♭7
Hirajoshi	1	2	♭3			5	♭6		
Japanese (b)	1	2			4	5	♭6		
Kumoi	1	2	♭3			5		6	
Pentatonic Major	1	2		3		5		6	
Pentatonic Neutral	1	2			4	5			♭7

6 Tone Scales

Scale						
Major Blues Scale	1	2	♭3	3	5	6

7 Tone Scales

Scale											
Aeolian	1	2	♭3		4		5	♭6		♭7	
Dorian	1	2	♭3		4		5		6	♭7	
Dorian ♯4	1	2	♭3			♯4	5		6	♭7	
Harmonic Minor	1	2	♭3		4		5	♭6			7
Hawaiian	1	2	♭3		4		5		6		7
Hindu	1	2		3	4		5	♭6		♭7	
Hungarian Minor	1	2	♭3			♯4	5	♭6			7
Lydian	1	2		3		♯4	5		6		7
Lydian Minor	1	2		3		♯4	5	♭6		♭7	
Lydian Diminished	1	2	♭3			♯4	5		6		7
Major (Ionian)	1	2		3	4		5		6		7
Melodic Minor (ascending)	1	2	♭3		4		5		6		7
Melodic Minor (descending)	1	2	♭3		4		5	♭6		♭7	
Mixolydian	1	2		3	4		5		6	♭7	
Roumanian Minor	1	2	♭3			♯4	5		6	♭7	

8 Tone Scales

Bebop Major	1		2		3	4		5	♯5	6		7
Bebop Minor	1		2	♭3	3	4		5		6	♭7	
Bebop Dominant	1		2		3	4		5		6	♭7	7
Japanese (Ichikosucho)	1		2		3	4	♯4	5		6		7
Jewish (Adonai Malakh)	1	♭2	2	♭3		4		5		6	♭7	

9 Tone Scales

Japanese (Taishikcho)	1		2		3	4	♯4	5		6	♯6	7
Nine Tone Scale	1		2	♯2	3		♯4	5	♯5	6		7

Suspended 4th
1 4 5

5 Tone Scales

Chinese 2	1		2			4		5		6		
Japanese (a)	1	♭2				4		5	♭6			
Japanese (b)	1		2			4		5	♭6			
Japanese (in sen)	1	♭2				4		5			♭7	
Kumoi 2	1	♭2				4		5	♭6			
Pentatonic Neutral	1		2			4		5			♭7	
Pentatonic Minor	1			♭3		4		5			♭7	

6 Tone Scales

Blues	1			♭3		4	♯4	5			♭7	

7 Tone Scales

Aeolian	1		2	♭3		4		5	♭6		♭7	
Blues Variation 1	1			♭3		4	♭5	5			♭7	7
Byzantine	1	♭2			3	4		5	♭6			7
Dorian	1		2	♭3		4		5		6	♭7	
Double Harmonic	1	♭2			3	4		5	♭6			7
Harmonic Minor	1		2	♭3		4		5	♭6			7
Hawaiian	1		2	♭3		4		5		6		7
Hindu	1		2		3	4		5	♭6		♭7	
Hungarian Gypsy Persian	1	♭2			3	4		5	♭6			7

Javanese	1	♭2		♭3		4		5		6	♭7	
Major (Ionian)	1		2		3	4		5		6		7
Melodic Minor (ascending)	1		2	♭3		4		5		6		7
Melodic Minor (descending)	1		2	♭3		4		5	♭6		♭7	
Mixolydian	1		2		3	4		5		6	♭7	
Mixo-Blues	1			♭3	3	4	♭5	5			♭7	
Mohammedan	1			♭3	3	4		5	♭6	6		7
Neopolitan	1	♭2		♭3		4		5	♭6			7
Neopolitan Major	1	♭2		♭3		4		5		6		7
Neopolitan Minor	1	♭2		♭3		4		5	♭6		♭7	
Phrygian	1	♭2		♭3		4		5	♭6		♭7	
Phrygian Major	1	♭2			3	4		5	♭6		♭7	
Spanish Gypsy	1	♭2			3	4		5	♭6		♭7	

8 Tone Scales

Bebop Major	1		2		3	4		5	♯5	6		7
Bebop Minor	1		2	♭3	3	4		5		6	♭7	
Bebop Dominant	1		2		3	4		5		6	♭7	7
Bebop Half-Diminished	1	♭2		♭3		4	♭5	5	♭6			7
Blues Variation 2	1			♭3	3	4	♭5	5			♭7	7
Japanese (Ichikosucho)	1		2		3	4	♯4	5		6		7
Jewish (Adonai Malakh)	1	♭2	2	♭3		4		5		6	♭7	

9 Tone Scales

Blues Variation 3	1			♭3	3	4	♭5	5		6	♭7	7
Japanese (Taishikcho)	1		2		3	4	♯4	5		6	♯6	7
Moorish Phrygian	1	♭2		♭3	3	4		5	♯5		♭7	7

9 ♭5

1 3 ♭5 7 9

7 Tone Scales

Leading Whole Tone	1		2		3		♯4		♯5		♯6	7
Lydian	1		2		3		♯4	5		6		7
Lydian Augmented	1		2		3		♯4		♯5	6		7

8 Tone Scales

Algerian	1		2	b3	3	4	#4		b6			7
Japanese (Ichikosucho)	1		2		3	4	#4	5		6		7

9 Tone Scales

Japanese (Taishikcho)	1		2		3	4	#4	5		6	#6	7
Nine Tone Scale	1		2	#2	3		#4	5	#5	6		7

9 #5

1 3 #5 b7 9

6 Tone Scales

Auxiliary Augmented	1		2		3		#4		#5		#6	
Whole Tone	1		2		3		#4		#5		b7	

7 Tone Scales

Arabian (b)	1		2		3	4	#4		#5		b7	
Hindu	1		2		3	4		5	b6		b7	
Hungarian Gypsy Persian	1	b2			3	4		5	b6			7
Leading Whole Tone	1		2		3		#4		#5		#6	7
Major Locrian	1		2		3	4	b5		b6		b7	

11 b9

1 5 b7 b9 11

5 Tone Scales

Japanese (in sen)	1	b2				4		5			b7	

7 Tone Scales

Javanese	1	b2		b3		4		5		6	b7	
Neopolitan Minor	1	b2		b3		4		5	b6		b7	
Phrygian	1	b2		b3		4		5	b6		b7	
Phrygian Major	1	b2			3	4		5	b6		b7	
Spanish Gypsy	1	b2			3	4		5	b6		b7	

8 Tone Scales

Jewish (Adonai Malakh) 1 b2 2 b3 4 5 6 b7

9 Tone Scales

Moorish Phrygian 1 b2 b3 3 4 5 #5 b7 7

13 b9

1 3 5 b7 b9 13

8 Tone Scales

Auxiliary Diminished Blues 1 b2 b3 3 b5 5 6 b7

13 #11

1 3 5 b7 9 #11 13

7 Tone Scales

Overtone Dominant 1 2 3 #4 5 6 b7

9 Tone Scales

Japanese (Taishikcho) 1 2 3 4 #4 5 6 #6 7

Chord Extensions

Key of A (OC)

A	A♯	B	C	C♯	D	D♯	E	F	F♯	G	G♯	A	A♯	B	C	C♯	D	D♯	E	F	F♯	G	G♯	A
12	11	10	9	8	7	6	5	4	3	2	1	0	1	2	3	4	5	6	7	8	9	10	11	12
OC		M2		M3	P4		P5		M6		M7	OC		M2		M3	P4		P5		M6		M7	OC
	m2		m3			D5		m6		m7			m2		m3			D5		m6		m7		
	♭9	9	♯9		11	♯11			13				♭9	9	♯9		11	♯11			13			

Key of A m2

A	A♯	B	C	C♯	D	D♯	E	F	F♯	G	G♯	A	A♯	B	C	C♯	D	D♯	E	F	F♯	G	G♯	A
12	11	10	9	8	7	6	5	4	3	2	1	0	1	2	3	4	5	6	7	8	9	10	11	12
	M2		M3	P4		P5		M6		M7	OC		M2		M3	P4		P5		M6		M7	OC	
m2		m3			D5		m6		m7			m2		m3			D5		m6		m7			m2
♭9	9	♯9		11	♯11			13				♭9	9	♯9		11	♯11			13				♭9

Key of A M2

A	A♯	B	C	C♯	D	D♯	E	F	F♯	G	G♯	A	A♯	B	C	C♯	D	D♯	E	F	F♯	G	G♯	A
12	11	10	9	8	7	6	5	4	3	2	1	0	1	2	3	4	5	6	7	8	9	10	11	12
M2		M3	P4		P5		M6		M7	OC		M2		M3	P4		P5		M6		M7	OC		M2
	m3			D5		m6		m7			m2		m3			D5		m6		m7			m2	
9	♯9		11	♯11			13				♭9	9	♯9		11	♯11			13				♭9	9

Key of A m3

A	A♯	B	C	C♯	D	D♯	E	F	F♯	G	G♯	A	A♯	B	C	C♯	D	D♯	E	F	F♯	G	G♯	A
12	11	10	9	8	7	6	5	4	3	2	1	0	1	2	3	4	5	6	7	8	9	10	11	12
	M3	P4		P5		M6		M7	OC		M2		M3	P4		P5		M6		M7	OC		M2	
m3			D5		m6		m7			m2		m3			D5		m6		m7			m2		m3
♯9		11	♯11			13				♭9	9	♯9		11	♯11			13				♭9	9	♯9

Key of A M3

A	A♯	B	C	C♯	D	D♯	E	F	F♯	G	G♯	A	A♯	B	C	C♯	D	D♯	E	F	F♯	G	G♯	A
12	11	10	9	8	7	6	5	4	3	2	1	0	1	2	3	4	5	6	7	8	9	10	11	12
M3	P4		P5		M6		M7	OC		M2		M3	P4		P5		M6		M7	OC		M2		M3
		D5		m6		m7			m2		m3			D5		m6		m7			m2		m3	
	11	♯11			13				♭9	9	♯9		11	♯11			13				♭9	9	♯9	

Key of A P4

A	A♯	B	C	C♯	D	D♯	E	F	F♯	G	G♯	A	A♯	B	C	C♯	D	D♯	E	F	F♯	G	G♯	A
12	11	10	9	8	7	6	5	4	3	2	1	0	1	2	3	4	5	6	7	8	9	10	11	12
P4		P5		M6		M7	OC		M2		M3	P4		P5		M6		M7	OC		M2		M3	P4
	D5		m6		m7			m2		m3			D5		m6		m7			m2		m3		
11	♯11			13				♭9	9	♯9		11	♯11			13				♭9	9	♯9		11

Key of A D5

A	A♯	B	C	C♯	D	D♯	E	F	F♯	G	G♯	A	A♯	B	C	C♯	D	D♯	E	F	F♯	G	G♯	A
12	11	10	9	8	7	6	5	4	3	2	1	0	1	2	3	4	5	6	7	8	9	10	11	12
	P5		M6		M7	OC		M2		M3	P4		P5		M6		M7	OC		M2		M3	P4	
D5		m6		m7			m2		m3			D5		m6		m7			m2		m3			D5
♯11			13				♭9	9	♯9		11	♯11			13				♭9	9	♯9		11	♯11

Key of A P5

A	A♯	B	C	C♯	D	D♯	E	F	F♯	G	G♯	A	A♯	B	C	C♯	D	D♯	E	F	F♯	G	G♯	A
12	11	10	9	8	7	6	5	4	3	2	1	0	1	2	3	4	5	6	7	8	9	10	11	12
P5		M6		M7	OC		M2		M3	P4		P5		M6		M7	OC		M2		M3	P4		P5
	m6		m7			m2		m3			D5		m6		m7			m2		m3			D5	
		13				♭9	9	♯9		11	♯11			13				♭9	9	♯9		11	♯11	

Key of A m6

A	A♯	B	C	C♯	D	D♯	E	F	F♯	G	G♯	A	A♯	B	C	C♯	D	D♯	E	F	F♯	G	G♯	A
12	11	10	9	8	7	6	5	4	3	2	1	0	1	2	3	4	5	6	7	8	9	10	11	12
	M6		M7	OC		M2		M3	P4		P5		M6		M7	OC		M2		M3	P4		P5	
m6		m7			m2		m3			D5		m6		m7			m2		m3			D5		m6
	13				♭9	9	♯9		11	♯11			13				♭9	9	♯9		11	♯11		

Key of A M6

A	A♯	B	C	C♯	D	D♯	E	F	F♯	G	G♯	A	A♯	B	C	C♯	D	D♯	E	F	F♯	G	G♯	A
12	**11**	**10**	**9**	**8**	**7**	**6**	**5**	**4**	**3**	**2**	**1**	**0**	**1**	**2**	**3**	**4**	**5**	**6**	**7**	**8**	**9**	**10**	**11**	**12**
M6		M7	OC		M2		M3	P4		P5		M6		M7	OC		M2		M3	P4		P5		M6
	m7			m2		m3			D5		m6		m7			m2		m3			D5		m6	
13				♭9	9	♯9		11	♯11			13				♭9	9	♯9		11	♯11			13

Key of A m7

A	A♯	B	C	C♯	D	D♯	E	F	F♯	G	G♯	A	A♯	B	C	C♯	D	D♯	E	F	F♯	G	G♯	A
12	**11**	**10**	**9**	**8**	**7**	**6**	**5**	**4**	**3**	**2**	**1**	**0**	**1**	**2**	**3**	**4**	**5**	**6**	**7**	**8**	**9**	**10**	**11**	**12**
	M7	OC		M2		M3	P4		P5		M6		M7	OC		M2		M3	P4		P5		M6	
m7			m2		m3			D5		m6		m7			m2		m3			D5		m6		m7
			♭9	9	♯9		11	♯11			13				♭9	9	♯9		11	♯11			13	

Key of A M7

A	A♯	B	C	C♯	D	D♯	E	F	F♯	G	G♯	A	A♯	B	C	C♯	D	D♯	E	F	F♯	G	G♯	A
12	**11**	**10**	**9**	**8**	**7**	**6**	**5**	**4**	**3**	**2**	**1**	**0**	**1**	**2**	**3**	**4**	**5**	**6**	**7**	**8**	**9**	**10**	**11**	**12**
M7	OC		M2		M3	P4		P5		M6		M7	OC		M2		M3	P4		P5		M6		M7
		m2		m3			D5		m6		m7			m2		m3			D5		m6		m7	
		♭9	9	♯9		11	♯11			13				♭9	9	♯9		11	♯11			13		

Key of A♯ (OC)

A♯	B	C	C♯	D	D♯	E	F	F♯	G	G♯	A	A♯	B	C	C♯	D	D♯	E	F	F♯	G	G♯	A	A♯
12	**11**	**10**	**9**	**8**	**7**	**6**	**5**	**4**	**3**	**2**	**1**	**0**	**1**	**2**	**3**	**4**	**5**	**6**	**7**	**8**	**9**	**10**	**11**	**12**
OC		M2		M3	P4		P5		M6		M7	OC		M2		M3	P4		P5		M6		M7	OC
	m2		m3			D5		m6		m7			m2		m3			D5		m6		m7		
	♭9	9	♯9		11	♯11			13				♭9	9	♯9		11	♯11			13			

Key of A♯ m2

A♯	B	C	C♯	D	D♯	E	F	F♯	G	G♯	A	A♯	B	C	C♯	D	D♯	E	F	F♯	G	G♯	A	A♯
12	**11**	**10**	**9**	**8**	**7**	**6**	**5**	**4**	**3**	**2**	**1**	**0**	**1**	**2**	**3**	**4**	**5**	**6**	**7**	**8**	**9**	**10**	**11**	**12**
	M2		M3	P4		P5		M6		M7	OC		M2		M3	P4		P5		M6		M7	OC	
m2		m3			D5		m6		m7			m2		m3			D5		m6		m7			m2
♭9	9	♯9		11	♯11			13				♭9	9	♯9		11	♯11			13				♭9

Key of A♯ M2

A♯	B	C	C♯	D	D♯	E	F	F♯	G	G♯	A	A♯	B	C	C♯	D	D♯	E	F	F♯	G	G♯	A	A♯
12	11	10	9	8	7	6	5	4	3	2	1	0	1	2	3	4	5	6	7	8	9	10	11	12
M2		M3	P4		P5		M6		M7	OC		M2		M3	P4		P5		M6		M7	OC		M2
	m3			D5		m6		m7			m2		m3			D5		m6		m7			m2	
9	♯9		11	♯11			13				♭9	9	♯9		11	♯11			13				♭9	9

Key of A♯ m3

A♯	B	C	C♯	D	D♯	E	F	F♯	G	G♯	A	A♯	B	C	C♯	D	D♯	E	F	F♯	G	G♯	A	A♯
12	11	10	9	8	7	6	5	4	3	2	1	0	1	2	3	4	5	6	7	8	9	10	11	12
	M3	P4		P5		M6		M7	OC		M2		M3	P4		P5		M6		M7	OC		M2	
m3			D5		m6		m7			m2		m3			D5		m6		m7			m2		m3
♯9		11	♯11			13				♭9	9	♯9		11	♯11			13				♭9	9	♯9

Key of A♯ M3

A♯	B	C	C♯	D	D♯	E	F	F♯	G	G♯	A	A♯	B	C	C♯	D	D♯	E	F	F♯	G	G♯	A	A♯
12	11	10	9	8	7	6	5	4	3	2	1	0	1	2	3	4	5	6	7	8	9	10	11	12
M3	P4		P5		M6		M7	OC		M2		M3	P4		P5		M6		M7	OC		M2		M3
		D5		m6		m7			m2		m3			D5		m6		m7			m2		m3	
	11	♯11			13				♭9	9	♯9		11	♯11			13				♭9	9	♯9	

Key of A♯ P4

A♯	B	C	C♯	D	D♯	E	F	F♯	G	G♯	A	A♯	B	C	C♯	D	D♯	E	F	F♯	G	G♯	A	A♯
12	11	10	9	8	7	6	5	4	3	2	1	0	1	2	3	4	5	6	7	8	9	10	11	12
P4		P5		M6		M7	OC		M2		M3	P4		P5		M6		M7	OC		M2		M3	P4
	D5		m6		m7			m2		m3			D5		m6		m7			m2		m3		
11	♯11			13				♭9	9	♯9		11	♯11			13				♭9	9	♯9		11

Key of A♯ D5

A♯	B	C	C♯	D	D♯	E	F	F♯	G	G♯	A	A♯	B	C	C♯	D	D♯	E	F	F♯	G	G♯	A	A♯
12	11	10	9	8	7	6	5	4	3	2	1	0	1	2	3	4	5	6	7	8	9	10	11	12
	P5		M6		M7	OC		M2		M3	P4		P5		M6		M7	OC		M2		M3	P4	
D5		m6		m7			m2		m3			D5		m6		m7			m2		m3			D5
♯11			13				♭9	9	♯9		11	♯11			13				♭9	9	♯9		11	♯11

Key of A♯ P5

A♯	B	C	C♯	D	D♯	E	F	F♯	G	G♯	A	A♯	B	C	C♯	D	D♯	E	F	F♯	G	G♯	A	A♯
12	11	10	9	8	7	6	5	4	3	2	1	0	1	2	3	4	5	6	7	8	9	10	11	12
P5		M6		M7	OC		M2		M3	P4		P5		M6		M7	OC		M2		M3	P4		P5
	m6		m7			m2		m3			D5		m6		m7			m2		m3			D5	
		13				♭9	9	♯9		11	♯11			13				♭9	9	♯9		11	♯11	

Key of A♯ m6

A♯	B	C	C♯	D	D♯	E	F	F♯	G	G♯	A	A♯	B	C	C♯	D	D♯	E	F	F♯	G	G♯	A	A♯
12	11	10	9	8	7	6	5	4	3	2	1	0	1	2	3	4	5	6	7	8	9	10	11	12
	M6		M7	OC		M2		M3	P4		P5		M6		M7	OC		M2		M3	P4		P5	
m6		m7			m2		m3			D5		m6		m7			m2		m3			D5		m6
	13				♭9	9	♯9		11	♯11			13				♭9	9	♯9		11	♯11		

Key of A♯ M6

A♯	B	C	C♯	D	D♯	E	F	F♯	G	G♯	A	A♯	B	C	C♯	D	D♯	E	F	F♯	G	G♯	A	A♯
12	11	10	9	8	7	6	5	4	3	2	1	0	1	2	3	4	5	6	7	8	9	10	11	12
M6		M7	OC		M2		M3	P4		P5		M6		M7	OC		M2		M3	P4		P5		M6
	m7			m2		m3			D5		m6		m7			m2		m3			D5		m6	
13				♭9	9	♯9		11	♯11			13				♭9	9	♯9		11	♯11			13

Key of A♯ m7

A♯	B	C	C♯	D	D♯	E	F	F♯	G	G♯	A	A♯	B	C	C♯	D	D♯	E	F	F♯	G	G♯	A	A♯
12	11	10	9	8	7	6	5	4	3	2	1	0	1	2	3	4	5	6	7	8	9	10	11	12
	M7	OC		M2		M3	P4		P5		M6		M7	OC		M2		M3	P4		P5		M6	
m7			m2		m3			D5		m6		m7			m2		m3			D5		m6		m7
			♭9	9	♯9		11	♯11			13				♭9	9	♯9		11	♯11			13	

Key of A♯ M7

A♯	B	C	C♯	D	D♯	E	F	F♯	G	G♯	A	A♯	B	C	C♯	D	D♯	E	F	F♯	G	G♯	A	A♯
12	11	10	9	8	7	6	5	4	3	2	1	0	1	2	3	4	5	6	7	8	9	10	11	12
M7	OC		M2		M3	P4		P5		M6		M7	OC		M2		M3	P4		P5		M6		M7
		m2		m3			D5		m6		m7			m2		m3			D5		m6		m7	
		♭9	9	♯9		11	♯11			13				♭9	9	♯9		11	♯11			13		

Key of B (OC)

B	C	C♯	D	D♯	E	F	F♯	G	G♯	A	A♯	B	C	C♯	D	D♯	E	F	F♯	G	G♯	A	A♯	B
12	**11**	**10**	**9**	**8**	**7**	**6**	**5**	**4**	**3**	**2**	**1**	**0**	**1**	**2**	**3**	**4**	**5**	**6**	**7**	**8**	**9**	**10**	**11**	**12**
OC		M2		M3	P4		P5		M6		M7	OC		M2		M3	P4		P5		M6		M7	OC
	m2		m3			D5		m6		m7			m2		m3			D5		m6		m7		
	♭9	9	♯9		11	♯11			13				♭9	9	♯9		11	♯11			13			

Key of B m2

B	C	C♯	D	D♯	E	F	F♯	G	G♯	A	A♯	B	C	C♯	D	D♯	E	F	F♯	G	G♯	A	A♯	B
12	**11**	**10**	**9**	**8**	**7**	**6**	**5**	**4**	**3**	**2**	**1**	**0**	**1**	**2**	**3**	**4**	**5**	**6**	**7**	**8**	**9**	**10**	**11**	**12**
	M2		M3	P4		P5		M6		M7	OC		M2		M3	P4		P5		M6		M7	OC	
m2		m3			D5		m6		m7			m2		m3			D5		m6		m7			m2
♭9	9	♯9		11	♯11			13				♭9	9	♯9		11	♯11			13				♭9

Key of B M2

B	C	C♯	D	D♯	E	F	F♯	G	G♯	A	A♯	B	C	C♯	D	D♯	E	F	F♯	G	G♯	A	A♯	B
12	**11**	**10**	**9**	**8**	**7**	**6**	**5**	**4**	**3**	**2**	**1**	**0**	**1**	**2**	**3**	**4**	**5**	**6**	**7**	**8**	**9**	**10**	**11**	**12**
M2		M3	P4		P5		M6		M7	OC		M2		M3	P4		P5		M6		M7	OC		M2
	m3			D5		m6		m7			m2		m3			D5		m6		m7			m2	
9	♯9		11	♯11			13				♭9	9	♯9		11	♯11			13				♭9	9

Key of B m3

B	C	C♯	D	D♯	E	F	F♯	G	G♯	A	A♯	B	C	C♯	D	D♯	E	F	F♯	G	G♯	A	A♯	B
12	**11**	**10**	**9**	**8**	**7**	**6**	**5**	**4**	**3**	**2**	**1**	**0**	**1**	**2**	**3**	**4**	**5**	**6**	**7**	**8**	**9**	**10**	**11**	**12**
	M3	P4		P5		M6		M7	OC		M2		M3	P4		P5		M6		M7	OC		M2	
m3			D5		m6		m7			m2		m3			D5		m6		m7			m2		m3
♯9		11	♯11			13				♭9	9	♯9		11	♯11			13				♭9	9	♯9

Key of B M3

B	C	C♯	D	D♯	E	F	F♯	G	G♯	A	A♯	B	C	C♯	D	D♯	E	F	F♯	G	G♯	A	A♯	B
12	**11**	**10**	**9**	**8**	**7**	**6**	**5**	**4**	**3**	**2**	**1**	**0**	**1**	**2**	**3**	**4**	**5**	**6**	**7**	**8**	**9**	**10**	**11**	**12**
M3	P4		P5		M6		M7	OC		M2		M3	P4		P5		M6		M7	OC		M2		M3
		D5		m6		m7			m2		m3			D5		m6		m7			m2		m3	
	11	♯11			13				♭9	9	♯9		11	♯11			13				♭9	9	♯9	

Key of B P4

B	C	C♯	D	D♯	E	F	F♯	G	G♯	A	A♯	B	C	C♯	D	D♯	E	F	F♯	G	G♯	A	A♯	B
12	11	10	9	8	7	6	5	4	3	2	1	0	1	2	3	4	5	6	7	8	9	10	11	12
P4		P5		M6		M7	OC		M2		M3	P4		P5		M6		M7	OC		M2		M3	P4
	D5		m6		m7			m2		m3			D5		m6		m7			m2		m3		
11	♯11			13				♭9	9	♯9		11	♯11			13				♭9	9	♯9		11

Key of B D5

B	C	C♯	D	D♯	E	F	F♯	G	G♯	A	A♯	B	C	C♯	D	D♯	E	F	F♯	G	G♯	A	A♯	B
12	11	10	9	8	7	6	5	4	3	2	1	0	1	2	3	4	5	6	7	8	9	10	11	12
	P5		M6		M7	OC		M2		M3	P4		P5		M6		M7	OC		M2		M3	P4	
D5		m6		m7			m2		m3			D5		m6		m7			m2		m3			D5
♯11			13				♭9	9	♯9		11	♯11			13				♭9	9	♯9		11	♯11

Key of B P5

B	C	C♯	D	D♯	E	F	F♯	G	G♯	A	A♯	B	C	C♯	D	D♯	E	F	F♯	G	G♯	A	A♯	B
12	11	10	9	8	7	6	5	4	3	2	1	0	1	2	3	4	5	6	7	8	9	10	11	12
P5		M6		M7	OC		M2		M3	P4		P5		M6		M7	OC		M2		M3	P4		P5
	m6		m7			m2		m3			D5		m6		m7			m2		m3			D5	
		13				♭9	9	♯9		11	♯11			13				♭9	9	♯9		11	♯11	

Key of B m6

B	C	C♯	D	D♯	E	F	F♯	G	G♯	A	A♯	B	C	C♯	D	D♯	E	F	F♯	G	G♯	A	A♯	B
12	11	10	9	8	7	6	5	4	3	2	1	0	1	2	3	4	5	6	7	8	9	10	11	12
	M6		M7	OC		M2		M3	P4		P5		M6		M7	OC		M2		M3	P4		P5	
m6		m7			m2		m3			D5		m6		m7			m2		m3			D5		m6
	13				♭9	9	♯9		11	♯11			13				♭9	9	♯9		11	♯11		

Key of B M6

B	C	C♯	D	D♯	E	F	F♯	G	G♯	A	A♯	B	C	C♯	D	D♯	E	F	F♯	G	G♯	A	A♯	B
12	11	10	9	8	7	6	5	4	3	2	1	0	1	2	3	4	5	6	7	8	9	10	11	12
M6		M7	OC		M2		M3	P4		P5		M6		M7	OC		M2		M3	P4		P5		M6
	m7			m2		m3			D5		m6		m7			m2		m3			D5		m6	
13				♭9	9	♯9		11	♯11			13				♭9	9	♯9		11	♯11			13

Key of B m7

B	C	C♯	D	D♯	E	F	F♯	G	G♯	A	A♯	B	C	C♯	D	D♯	E	F	F♯	G	G♯	A	A♯	B
12	**11**	**10**	**9**	**8**	**7**	**6**	**5**	**4**	**3**	**2**	**1**	**0**	**1**	**2**	**3**	**4**	**5**	**6**	**7**	**8**	**9**	**10**	**11**	**12**
	M7	OC		M2		M3	P4		P5		M6		M7	OC		M2		M3	P4		P5		M6	
m7			m2		m3			D5		m6		m7			m2		m3			D5		m6		m7
			♭9	9	♯9		11	♯11			13				♭9	9	♯9		11	♯11			13	

Key of B M7

B	C	C♯	D	D♯	E	F	F♯	G	G♯	A	A♯	B	C	C♯	D	D♯	E	F	F♯	G	G♯	A	A♯	B
12	**11**	**10**	**9**	**8**	**7**	**6**	**5**	**4**	**3**	**2**	**1**	**0**	**1**	**2**	**3**	**4**	**5**	**6**	**7**	**8**	**9**	**10**	**11**	**12**
M7	OC		M2		M3	P4		P5		M6		M7	OC		M2		M3	P4		P5		M6		M7
		m2		m3			D5		m6		m7			m2		m3			D5		m6		m7	
		♭9	9	♯9		11	♯11			13				♭9	9	♯9		11	♯11			13		

Key of C (OC)

C	C♯	D	D♯	E	F	F♯	G	G♯	A	A♯	B	C	C♯	D	D♯	E	F	F♯	G	G♯	A	A♯	B	C
12	**11**	**10**	**9**	**8**	**7**	**6**	**5**	**4**	**3**	**2**	**1**	**0**	**1**	**2**	**3**	**4**	**5**	**6**	**7**	**8**	**9**	**10**	**11**	**12**
OC		M2		M3	P4		P5		M6		M7	OC		M2		M3	P4		P5		M6		M7	OC
	m2		m3			D5		m6		m7			m2		m3			D5		m6		m7		
	♭9	9	♯9		11	♯11			13				♭9	9	♯9		11	♯11			13			

Key of C m2

C	C♯	D	D♯	E	F	F♯	G	G♯	A	A♯	B	C	C♯	D	D♯	E	F	F♯	G	G♯	A	A♯	B	C
12	**11**	**10**	**9**	**8**	**7**	**6**	**5**	**4**	**3**	**2**	**1**	**0**	**1**	**2**	**3**	**4**	**5**	**6**	**7**	**8**	**9**	**10**	**11**	**12**
	M2		M3	P4		P5		M6		M7	OC		M2		M3	P4		P5		M6		M7	OC	
m2		m3			D5		m6		m7			m2		m3			D5		m6		m7			m2
♭9	9	♯9		11	♯11			13				♭9	9	♯9		11	♯11			13				♭9

Key of C M2

C	C♯	D	D♯	E	F	F♯	G	G♯	A	A♯	B	C	C♯	D	D♯	E	F	F♯	G	G♯	A	A♯	B	C
12	**11**	**10**	**9**	**8**	**7**	**6**	**5**	**4**	**3**	**2**	**1**	**0**	**1**	**2**	**3**	**4**	**5**	**6**	**7**	**8**	**9**	**10**	**11**	**12**
M2		M3	P4		P5		M6		M7	OC		M2		M3	P4		P5		M6		M7	OC		M2
	m3			D5		m6		m7			m2		m3			D5		m6		m7			m2	
9	♯9		11	♯11			13				♭9	9	♯9		11	♯11			13				♭9	9

Key of C m3

C	C♯	D	D♯	E	F	F♯	G	G♯	A	A♯	B	C	C♯	D	D♯	E	F	F♯	G	G♯	A	A♯	B	C
12	11	10	9	8	7	6	5	4	3	2	1	0	1	2	3	4	5	6	7	8	9	10	11	12
	M3	P4		P5		M6		M7	OC		M2		M3	P4		P5		M6		M7	OC		M2	
m3			D5		m6		m7			m2		m3			D5		m6		m7			m2		m3
♯9		11	♯11			13				♭9	9	♯9		11	♯11			13				♭9	9	♯9

Key of C M3

C	C♯	D	D♯	E	F	F♯	G	G♯	A	A♯	B	C	C♯	D	D♯	E	F	F♯	G	G♯	A	A♯	B	C
12	11	10	9	8	7	6	5	4	3	2	1	0	1	2	3	4	5	6	7	8	9	10	11	12
M3	P4		P5		M6		M7	OC		M2		M3	P4		P5		M6		M7	OC		M2		M3
		D5		m6		m7			m2		m3			D5		m6		m7			m2		m3	
	11	♯11			13				♭9	9	♯9		11	♯11			13				♭9	9	♯9	

Key of C P4

C	C♯	D	D♯	E	F	F♯	G	G♯	A	A♯	B	C	C♯	D	D♯	E	F	F♯	G	G♯	A	A♯	B	C
12	11	10	9	8	7	6	5	4	3	2	1	0	1	2	3	4	5	6	7	8	9	10	11	12
P4		P5		M6		M7	OC		M2		M3	P4		P5		M6		M7	OC		M2		M3	P4
	D5		m6		m7			m2		m3			D5		m6		m7			m2		m3		
11	♯11			13				♭9	9	♯9		11	♯11			13				♭9	9	♯9		11

Key of C D5

C	C♯	D	D♯	E	F	F♯	G	G♯	A	A♯	B	C	C♯	D	D♯	E	F	F♯	G	G♯	A	A♯	B	C
12	11	10	9	8	7	6	5	4	3	2	1	0	1	2	3	4	5	6	7	8	9	10	11	12
	P5		M6		M7	OC		M2		M3	P4		P5		M6		M7	OC		M2		M3	P4	
D5		m6		m7			m2		m3			D5		m6		m7			m2		m3			D5
♯11			13				♭9	9	♯9		11	♯11			13				♭9	9	♯9		11	♯11

Key of C P5

C	C♯	D	D♯	E	F	F♯	G	G♯	A	A♯	B	C	C♯	D	D♯	E	F	F♯	G	G♯	A	A♯	B	C
12	11	10	9	8	7	6	5	4	3	2	1	0	1	2	3	4	5	6	7	8	9	10	11	12
P5		M6		M7	OC		M2		M3	P4		P5		M6		M7	OC		M2		M3	P4		P5
	m6		m7			m2		m3			D5		m6		m7			m2		m3			D5	
		13				♭9	9	♯9		11	♯11			13				♭9	9	♯9		11	♯11	

Key of C m6

C	C♯	D	D♯	E	F	F♯	G	G♯	A	A♯	B	C	C♯	D	D♯	E	F	F♯	G	G♯	A	A♯	B	C
12	11	10	9	8	7	6	5	4	3	2	1	0	1	2	3	4	5	6	7	8	9	10	11	12
	M6		M7	OC		M2		M3	P4		P5		M6		M7	OC		M2		M3	P4		P5	
m6		m7			m2		m3			D5		m6		m7			m2		m3			D5		m6
	13				♭9	9	♯9		11	♯11			13				♭9	9	♯9		11	♯11		

Key of C M6

C	C♯	D	D♯	E	F	F♯	G	G♯	A	A♯	B	C	C♯	D	D♯	E	F	F♯	G	G♯	A	A♯	B	C
12	11	10	9	8	7	6	5	4	3	2	1	0	1	2	3	4	5	6	7	8	9	10	11	12
M6		M7	OC		M2		M3	P4		P5		M6		M7	OC		M2		M3	P4		P5		M6
	m7			m2		m3			D5		m6		m7			m2		m3			D5		m6	
13				♭9	9	♯9		11	♯11			13				♭9	9	♯9		11	♯11			13

Key of C m7

C	C♯	D	D♯	E	F	F♯	G	G♯	A	A♯	B	C	C♯	D	D♯	E	F	F♯	G	G♯	A	A♯	B	C
12	11	10	9	8	7	6	5	4	3	2	1	0	1	2	3	4	5	6	7	8	9	10	11	12
	M7	OC		M2		M3	P4		P5		M6		M7	OC		M2		M3	P4		P5		M6	
m7			m2		m3			D5		m6		m7			m2		m3			D5		m6		m7
			♭9	9	♯9		11	♯11			13				♭9	9	♯9		11	♯11			13	

Key of C M7

C	C♯	D	D♯	E	F	F♯	G	G♯	A	A♯	B	C	C♯	D	D♯	E	F	F♯	G	G♯	A	A♯	B	C
12	11	10	9	8	7	6	5	4	3	2	1	0	1	2	3	4	5	6	7	8	9	10	11	12
M7	OC		M2		M3	P4		P5		M6		M7	OC		M2		M3	P4		P5		M6		M7
		m2		m3			D5		m6		m7			m2		m3			D5		m6		m7	
		♭9	9	♯9		11	♯11			13				♭9	9	♯9		11	♯11			13		

Key of C♯ (OC)

C♯	D	D♯	E	F	F♯	G	G♯	A	A♯	B	C	C♯	D	D♯	E	F	F♯	G	G♯	A	A♯	B	C	C♯
12	11	10	9	8	7	6	5	4	3	2	1	0	1	2	3	4	5	6	7	8	9	10	11	12
OC		M2		M3	P4		P5		M6		M7	OC		M2		M3	P4		P5		M6		M7	OC
	m2		m3			D5		m6		m7			m2		m3			D5		m6		m7		
	♭9	9	♯9		11	♯11			13				♭9	9	♯9		11	♯11			13			

Key of C♯ m2

C♯	D	D♯	E	F	F♯	G	G♯	A	A♯	B	C	C♯	D	D♯	E	F	F♯	G	G♯	A	A♯	B	C	C♯
12	**11**	**10**	**9**	**8**	**7**	**6**	**5**	**4**	**3**	**2**	**1**	**0**	**1**	**2**	**3**	**4**	**5**	**6**	**7**	**8**	**9**	**10**	**11**	**12**
	M2		M3	P4		P5		M6		M7	OC		M2		M3	P4		P5		M6		M7	OC	
m2		m3			D5		m6		m7			m2		m3			D5		m6		m7			m2
♭9	9	♯9		11	♯11			13				♭9	9	♯9		11	♯11			13				♭9

Key of C♯ M2

C♯	D	D♯	E	F	F♯	G	G♯	A	A♯	B	C	C♯	D	D♯	E	F	F♯	G	G♯	A	A♯	B	C	C♯
12	**11**	**10**	**9**	**8**	**7**	**6**	**5**	**4**	**3**	**2**	**1**	**0**	**1**	**2**	**3**	**4**	**5**	**6**	**7**	**8**	**9**	**10**	**11**	**12**
M2		M3	P4		P5		M6		M7	OC		M2		M3	P4		P5		M6		M7	OC		M2
	m3			D5		m6		m7			m2		m3			D5		m6		m7			m2	
9	♯9		11	♯11			13				♭9	9	♯9		11	♯11			13				♭9	9

Key of C♯ m3

C♯	D	D♯	E	F	F♯	G	G♯	A	A♯	B	C	C♯	D	D♯	E	F	F♯	G	G♯	A	A♯	B	C	C♯
12	**11**	**10**	**9**	**8**	**7**	**6**	**5**	**4**	**3**	**2**	**1**	**0**	**1**	**2**	**3**	**4**	**5**	**6**	**7**	**8**	**9**	**10**	**11**	**12**
	M3	P4		P5		M6		M7	OC		M2		M3	P4		P5		M6		M7	OC		M2	
m3			D5		m6		m7			m2		m3			D5		m6		m7			m2		m3
♯9		11	♯11			13				♭9	9	♯9		11	♯11			13				♭9	9	♯9

Key of C♯ M3

C♯	D	D♯	E	F	F♯	G	G♯	A	A♯	B	C	C♯	D	D♯	E	F	F♯	G	G♯	A	A♯	B	C	C♯
12	**11**	**10**	**9**	**8**	**7**	**6**	**5**	**4**	**3**	**2**	**1**	**0**	**1**	**2**	**3**	**4**	**5**	**6**	**7**	**8**	**9**	**10**	**11**	**12**
M3	P4		P5		M6		M7	OC		M2		M3	P4		P5		M6		M7	OC		M2		M3
		D5		m6		m7			m2		m3			D5		m6		m7			m2		m3	
	11	♯11			13				♭9	9	♯9		11	♯11			13				♭9	9	♯9	

Key of C♯ P4

C♯	D	D♯	E	F	F♯	G	G♯	A	A♯	B	C	C♯	D	D♯	E	F	F♯	G	G♯	A	A♯	B	C	C♯
12	**11**	**10**	**9**	**8**	**7**	**6**	**5**	**4**	**3**	**2**	**1**	**0**	**1**	**2**	**3**	**4**	**5**	**6**	**7**	**8**	**9**	**10**	**11**	**12**
P4		P5		M6		M7	OC		M2		M3	P4		P5		M6		M7	OC		M2		M3	P4
	D5		m6		m7			m2		m3			D5		m6		m7			m2		m3		
11	♯11			13				♭9	9	♯9		11	♯11		13					♭9	9	♯9		11

Key of C♯ D5

C♯	D	D♯	E	F	F♯	G	G♯	A	A♯	B	C	C♯	D	D♯	E	F	F♯	G	G♯	A	A♯	B	C	C♯
12	11	10	9	8	7	6	5	4	3	2	1	0	1	2	3	4	5	6	7	8	9	10	11	12
	P5		M6		M7	OC		M2		M3	P4		P5		M6		M7	OC		M2		M3	P4	
D5		m6		m7			m2		m3			D5		m6		m7			m2		m3			D5
♯11			13				♭9	9	♯9		11	♯11			13				♭9	9	♯9		11	♯11

Key of C♯ P5

C♯	D	D♯	E	F	F♯	G	G♯	A	A♯	B	C	C♯	D	D♯	E	F	F♯	G	G♯	A	A♯	B	C	C♯
12	11	10	9	8	7	6	5	4	3	2	1	0	1	2	3	4	5	6	7	8	9	10	11	12
P5		M6		M7	OC		M2		M3	P4		P5		M6		M7	OC		M2		M3	P4		P5
	m6		m7			m2		m3			D5		m6		m7			m2		m3			D5	
		13				♭9	9	♯9		11	♯11			13				♭9	9	♯9		11	♯11	

Key of C♯ m6

C♯	D	D♯	E	F	F♯	G	G♯	A	A♯	B	C	C♯	D	D♯	E	F	F♯	G	G♯	A	A♯	B	C	C♯
12	11	10	9	8	7	6	5	4	3	2	1	0	1	2	3	4	5	6	7	8	9	10	11	12
	M6		M7	OC		M2		M3	P4		P5		M6		M7	OC		M2		M3	P4		P5	
m6		m7			m2		m3			D5		m6		m7			m2		m3			D5		m6
	13				♭9	9	♯9		11	♯11			13				♭9	9	♯9		11	♯11		

Key of C♯ M6

C♯	D	D♯	E	F	F♯	G	G♯	A	A♯	B	C	C♯	D	D♯	E	F	F♯	G	G♯	A	A♯	B	C	C♯
12	11	10	9	8	7	6	5	4	3	2	1	0	1	2	3	4	5	6	7	8	9	10	11	12
M6		M7	OC		M2		M3	P4		P5		M6		M7	OC		M2		M3	P4		P5		M6
	m7			m2		m3			D5		m6		m7			m2		m3			D5		m6	
13				♭9	9	♯9		11	♯11			13				♭9	9	♯9		11	♯11			13

Key of C♯ m7

C♯	D	D♯	E	F	F♯	G	G♯	A	A♯	B	C	C♯	D	D♯	E	F	F♯	G	G♯	A	A♯	B	C	C♯
12	11	10	9	8	7	6	5	4	3	2	1	0	1	2	3	4	5	6	7	8	9	10	11	12
	M7	OC		M2		M3	P4		P5		M6		M7	OC		M2		M3	P4		P5		M6	
m7			m2		m3			D5		m6		m7			m2		m3			D5		m6		m7
			♭9	9	♯9		11	♯11			13				♭9	9	♯9		11	♯11			13	

Key of C♯ M7

C♯	D	D♯	E	F	F♯	G	G♯	A	A♯	B	C	C♯	D	D♯	E	F	F♯	G	G♯	A	A♯	B	C	C♯
12	11	10	9	8	7	6	5	4	3	2	1	0	1	2	3	4	5	6	7	8	9	10	11	12
M7	OC		M2		M3	P4		P5		M6		M7	OC		M2		M3	P4		P5		M6		M7
		m2		m3			D5		m6		m7			m2		m3			D5		m6		m7	
		♭9	9	♯9		11	♯11			13				♭9	9	♯9		11	♯11			13		

Key of D (OC)

D	D♯	E	F	F♯	G	G♯	A	A♯	B	C	C♯	D	D♯	E	F	F♯	G	G♯	A	A♯	B	C	C♯	D
12	11	10	9	8	7	6	5	4	3	2	1	0	1	2	3	4	5	6	7	8	9	10	11	12
OC		M2		M3	P4		P5		M6		M7	OC		M2		M3	P4		P5		M6		M7	OC
	m2		m3			D5		m6		m7			m2		m3			D5		m6		m7		
	♭9	9	♯9		11	♯11			13				♭9	9	♯9		11	♯11			13			

Key of D m2

D	D♯	E	F	F♯	G	G♯	A	A♯	B	C	C♯	D	D♯	E	F	F♯	G	G♯	A	A♯	B	C	C♯	D
12	11	10	9	8	7	6	5	4	3	2	1	0	1	2	3	4	5	6	7	8	9	10	11	12
	M2		M3	P4		P5		M6		M7	OC		M2		M3	P4		P5		M6		M7	OC	
m2		m3			D5		m6		m7			m2		m3			D5		m6		m7			m2
♭9	9	♯9		11	♯11			13				♭9	9	♯9		11	♯11			13				♭9

Key of D M2

D	D♯	E	F	F♯	G	G♯	A	A♯	B	C	C♯	D	D♯	E	F	F♯	G	G♯	A	A♯	B	C	C♯	D
12	11	10	9	8	7	6	5	4	3	2	1	0	1	2	3	4	5	6	7	8	9	10	11	12
M2		M3	P4		P5		M6		M7	OC		M2		M3	P4		P5		M6		M7	OC		M2
	m3			D5		m6		m7			m2		m3			D5		m6		m7			m2	
9	♯9		11	♯11		13					♭9	9	♯9		11	♯11		13					♭9	9

Key of D m3

D	D♯	E	F	F♯	G	G♯	A	A♯	B	C	C♯	D	D♯	E	F	F♯	G	G♯	A	A♯	B	C	C♯	D
12	11	10	9	8	7	6	5	4	3	2	1	0	1	2	3	4	5	6	7	8	9	10	11	12
	M3	P4		P5		M6		M7	OC		M2		M3	P4		P5		M6		M7	OC		M2	
m3			D5		m6		m7			m2		m3			D5		m6		m7			m2		m3
♯9		11	♯11		13					♭9	9	♯9		11	♯11		13					♭9	9	♯9

Key of D M3

D	D♯	E	F	F♯	G	G♯	A	A♯	B	C	C♯	D	D♯	E	F	F♯	G	G♯	A	A♯	B	C	C♯	D
12	11	10	9	8	7	6	5	4	3	2	1	0	1	2	3	4	5	6	7	8	9	10	11	12
M3	P4		P5		M6		M7	OC		M2		M3	P4		P5		M6		M7	OC		M2		M3
		D5		m6		m7			m2		m3			D5		m6		m7			m2		m3	
	11	♯11			13				♭9	9	♯9		11	♯11			13				♭9	9	♯9	

Key of D P4

D	D♯	E	F	F♯	G	G♯	A	A♯	B	C	C♯	D	D♯	E	F	F♯	G	G♯	A	A♯	B	C	C♯	D
12	11	10	9	8	7	6	5	4	3	2	1	0	1	2	3	4	5	6	7	8	9	10	11	12
P4		P5		M6		M7	OC		M2		M3	P4		P5		M6		M7	OC		M2		M3	P4
	D5		m6		m7			m2		m3			D5		m6		m7			m2		m3		
11	♯11			13				♭9	9	♯9		11	♯11			13				♭9	9	♯9		11

Key of D D5

D	D♯	E	F	F♯	G	G♯	A	A♯	B	C	C♯	D	D♯	E	F	F♯	G	G♯	A	A♯	B	C	C♯	D
12	11	10	9	8	7	6	5	4	3	2	1	0	1	2	3	4	5	6	7	8	9	10	11	12
	P5		M6		M7	OC		M2		M3	P4		P5		M6		M7	OC		M2		M3	P4	
D5		m6		m7			m2		m3			D5		m6		m7			m2		m3			D5
♯11			13				♭9	9	♯9		11	♯11			13				♭9	9	♯9		11	♯11

Key of D P5

D	D♯	E	F	F♯	G	G♯	A	A♯	B	C	C♯	D	D♯	E	F	F♯	G	G♯	A	A♯	B	C	C♯	D
12	11	10	9	8	7	6	5	4	3	2	1	0	1	2	3	4	5	6	7	8	9	10	11	12
P5		M6		M7	OC		M2		M3	P4		P5		M6		M7	OC		M2		M3	P4		P5
	m6		m7			m2		m3			D5		m6		m7			m2		m3			D5	
		13				♭9	9	♯9		11	♯11			13				♭9	9	♯9		11	♯11	

Key of D m6

D	D♯	E	F	F♯	G	G♯	A	A♯	B	C	C♯	D	D♯	E	F	F♯	G	G♯	A	A♯	B	C	C♯	D
12	11	10	9	8	7	6	5	4	3	2	1	0	1	2	3	4	5	6	7	8	9	10	11	12
	M6		M7	OC		M2		M3	P4		P5		M6		M7	OC		M2		M3	P4		P5	
m6		m7			m2		m3			D5		m6		m7			m2		m3			D5		m6
	13				♭9	9	♯9		11	♯11			13				♭9	9	♯9		11	♯11		

Key of D M6

D	D♯	E	F	F♯	G	G♯	A	A♯	B	C	C♯	D	D♯	E	F	F♯	G	G♯	A	A♯	B	C	C♯	D
12	11	10	9	8	7	6	5	4	3	2	1	0	1	2	3	4	5	6	7	8	9	10	11	12
M6		M7	OC		M2		M3	P4		P5		M6		M7	OC		M2		M3	P4		P5		M6
	m7			m2		m3			D5		m6		m7			m2		m3			D5		m6	
13				♭9	9	♯9		11	♯11			13				♭9	9	♯9		11	♯11			13

Key of D m7

D	D♯	E	F	F♯	G	G♯	A	A♯	B	C	C♯	D	D♯	E	F	F♯	G	G♯	A	A♯	B	C	C♯	D
12	11	10	9	8	7	6	5	4	3	2	1	0	1	2	3	4	5	6	7	8	9	10	11	12
	M7	OC		M2		M3	P4		P5		M6		M7	OC		M2		M3	P4		P5		M6	
m7			m2		m3			D5		m6		m7			m2		m3			D5		m6		m7
			♭9	9	♯9		11	♯11			13				♭9	9	♯9		11	♯11			13	

Key of D M7

D	D♯	E	F	F♯	G	G♯	A	A♯	B	C	C♯	D	D♯	E	F	F♯	G	G♯	A	A♯	B	C	C♯	D
12	11	10	9	8	7	6	5	4	3	2	1	0	1	2	3	4	5	6	7	8	9	10	11	12
M7	OC		M2		M3	P4		P5		M6		M7	OC		M2		M3	P4		P5		M6		M7
		m2		m3			D5		m6		m7			m2		m3			D5		m6		m7	
		♭9	9	♯9		11	♯11			13				♭9	9	♯9		11	♯11			13		

Key of D♯ (OC)

D♯	E	F	F♯	G	G♯	A	A♯	B	C	C♯	D	D♯	E	F	F♯	G	G♯	A	A♯	B	C	C♯	D	D♯
12	11	10	9	8	7	6	5	4	3	2	1	0	1	2	3	4	5	6	7	8	9	10	11	12
OC		M2		M3	P4		P5		M6		M7	OC		M2		M3	P4		P5		M6		M7	OC
	m2		m3			D5		m6		m7			m2		m3			D5		m6		m7		
	♭9	9	♯9		11	♯11			13				♭9	9	♯9		11	♯11			13			

Key of D♯ m2

D♯	E	F	F♯	G	G♯	A	A♯	B	C	C♯	D	D♯	E	F	F♯	G	G♯	A	A♯	B	C	C♯	D	D♯
12	11	10	9	8	7	6	5	4	3	2	1	0	1	2	3	4	5	6	7	8	9	10	11	12
	M2		M3	P4		P5		M6		M7	OC		M2		M3	P4		P5		M6		M7	OC	
m2		m3			D5		m6		m7			m2		m3			D5		m6		m7			m2
♭9	9	♯9		11	♯11			13				♭9	9	♯9		11	♯11			13				♭9

Key of D♯ M2

D♯	E	F	F♯	G	G♯	A	A♯	B	C	C♯	D	D♯	E	F	F♯	G	G♯	A	A♯	B	C	C♯	D	D♯
12	11	10	9	8	7	6	5	4	3	2	1	0	1	2	3	4	5	6	7	8	9	10	11	12
M2		M3	P4		P5		M6		M7	OC		M2		M3	P4		P5		M6		M7	OC		M2
	m3			D5		m6		m7			m2		m3			D5		m6		m7			m2	
9	♯9		11	♯11			13				♭9	9	♯9		11	♯11			13				♭9	9

Key of D♯ m3

D♯	E	F	F♯	G	G♯	A	A♯	B	C	C♯	D	D♯	E	F	F♯	G	G♯	A	A♯	B	C	C♯	D	D♯
12	11	10	9	8	7	6	5	4	3	2	1	0	1	2	3	4	5	6	7	8	9	10	11	12
	M3	P4		P5		M6		M7	OC		M2		M3	P4		P5		M6		M7	OC		M2	
m3			D5		m6		m7			m2		m3			D5		m6		m7			m2		m3
♯9		11	♯11			13				♭9	9	♯9		11	♯11			13				♭9	9	♯9

Key of D♯ M3

D♯	E	F	F♯	G	G♯	A	A♯	B	C	C♯	D	D♯	E	F	F♯	G	G♯	A	A♯	B	C	C♯	D	D♯
12	11	10	9	8	7	6	5	4	3	2	1	0	1	2	3	4	5	6	7	8	9	10	11	12
M3	P4		P5		M6		M7	OC		M2		M3	P4		P5		M6		M7	OC		M2		M3
		D5		m6		m7			m2		m3			D5		m6		m7			m2		m3	
	11	♯11			13				♭9	9	♯9		11	♯11			13				♭9	9	♯9	

Key of D♯ P4

D♯	E	F	F♯	G	G♯	A	A♯	B	C	C♯	D	D♯	E	F	F♯	G	G♯	A	A♯	B	C	C♯	D	D♯
12	11	10	9	8	7	6	5	4	3	2	1	0	1	2	3	4	5	6	7	8	9	10	11	12
P4		P5		M6		M7	OC		M2		M3	P4		P5		M6		M7	OC		M2		M3	P4
	D5		m6		m7			m2		m3			D5		m6		m7			m2		m3		
11	♯11			13				♭9	9	♯9		11	♯11			13				♭9	9	♯9		11

Key of D♯ D5

D♯	E	F	F♯	G	G♯	A	A♯	B	C	C♯	D	D♯	E	F	F♯	G	G♯	A	A♯	B	C	C♯	D	D♯
12	11	10	9	8	7	6	5	4	3	2	1	0	1	2	3	4	5	6	7	8	9	10	11	12
	P5		M6		M7	OC		M2		M3	P4		P5		M6		M7	OC		M2		M3	P4	
D5		m6		m7			m2		m3			D5		m6		m7			m2		m3			D5
♯11			13				♭9	9	♯9		11	♯11			13				♭9	9	♯9		11	♯11

Key of D♯ P5

D♯	E	F	F♯	G	G♯	A	A♯	B	C	C♯	D	D♯	E	F	F♯	G	G♯	A	A♯	B	C	C♯	D	D♯
12	11	10	9	8	7	6	5	4	3	2	1	0	1	2	3	4	5	6	7	8	9	10	11	12
P5		M6		M7	OC		M2		M3	P4		P5		M6		M7	OC		M2		M3	P4		P5
	m6		m7			m2		m3			D5		m6		m7			m2		m3			D5	
		13				♭9	9	♯9		11	♯11			13				♭9	9	♯9		11	♯11	

Key of D♯ m6

D♯	E	F	F♯	G	G♯	A	A♯	B	C	C♯	D	D♯	E	F	F♯	G	G♯	A	A♯	B	C	C♯	D	D♯
12	11	10	9	8	7	6	5	4	3	2	1	0	1	2	3	4	5	6	7	8	9	10	11	12
	M6		M7	OC		M2		M3	P4		P5		M6		M7	OC		M2		M3	P4		P5	
m6		m7			m2		m3			D5		m6		m7			m2		m3			D5		m6
	13				♭9	9	♯9		11	♯11			13				♭9	9	♯9		11	♯11		

Key of D♯ M6

D♯	E	F	F♯	G	G♯	A	A♯	B	C	C♯	D	D♯	E	F	F♯	G	G♯	A	A♯	B	C	C♯	D	D♯
12	11	10	9	8	7	6	5	4	3	2	1	0	1	2	3	4	5	6	7	8	9	10	11	12
M6		M7	OC		M2		M3	P4		P5		M6		M7	OC		M2		M3	P4		P5		M6
	m7			m2		m3			D5		m6		m7			m2		m3			D5		m6	
13				♭9	9	♯9		11	♯11			13				♭9	9	♯9		11	♯11			13

Key of D♯ m7

D♯	E	F	F♯	G	G♯	A	A♯	B	C	C♯	D	D♯	E	F	F♯	G	G♯	A	A♯	B	C	C♯	D	D♯
12	11	10	9	8	7	6	5	4	3	2	1	0	1	2	3	4	5	6	7	8	9	10	11	12
	M7	OC		M2		M3	P4		P5		M6		M7	OC		M2		M3	P4		P5		M6	
m7			m2		m3			D5		m6		m7			m2		m3			D5		m6		m7
			♭9	9	♯9		11	♯11			13				♭9	9	♯9		11	♯11			13	

Key of D♯ M7

D♯	E	F	F♯	G	G♯	A	A♯	B	C	C♯	D	D♯	E	F	F♯	G	G♯	A	A♯	B	C	C♯	D	D♯
12	11	10	9	8	7	6	5	4	3	2	1	0	1	2	3	4	5	6	7	8	9	10	11	12
M7	OC		M2		M3	P4		P5		M6		M7	OC		M2		M3	P4		P5		M6		M7
		m2		m3			D5		m6		m7			m2		m3			D5		m6		m7	
		♭9	9	♯9		11	♯11			13				♭9	9	♯9		11	♯11			13		

Key of E (OC)

E	F	F♯	G	G♯	A	A♯	B	C	C♯	D	D♯	E	F	F♯	G	G♯	A	A♯	B	C	C♯	D	D♯	E
12	11	10	9	8	7	6	5	4	3	2	1	0	1	2	3	4	5	6	7	8	9	10	11	12
OC		M2		M3	P4		P5		M6		M7	OC		M2		M3	P4		P5		M6		M7	OC
	m2		m3			D5		m6		m7			m2		m3			D5		m6		m7		
	♭9	9	♯9		11	♯11			13				♭9	9	♯9		11	♯11			13			

Key of E m2

E	F	F♯	G	G♯	A	A♯	B	C	C♯	D	D♯	E	F	F♯	G	G♯	A	A♯	B	C	C♯	D	D♯	E
12	11	10	9	8	7	6	5	4	3	2	1	0	1	2	3	4	5	6	7	8	9	10	11	12
	M2		M3	P4		P5		M6		M7	OC		M2		M3	P4		P5		M6		M7	OC	
m2		m3			D5		m6		m7			m2		m3			D5		m6		m7			m2
♭9	9	♯9		11	♯11			13				♭9	9	♯9		11	♯11			13				♭9

Key of E M2

E	F	F♯	G	G♯	A	A♯	B	C	C♯	D	D♯	E	F	F♯	G	G♯	A	A♯	B	C	C♯	D	D♯	E
12	11	10	9	8	7	6	5	4	3	2	1	0	1	2	3	4	5	6	7	8	9	10	11	12
M2		M3	P4		P5		M6		M7	OC		M2		M3	P4		P5		M6		M7	OC		M2
	m3			D5		m6		m7			m2		m3			D5		m6		m7			m2	
9	♯9		11	♯11			13				♭9	9	♯9		11	♯11			13				♭9	9

Key of E m3

E	F	F♯	G	G♯	A	A♯	B	C	C♯	D	D♯	E	F	F♯	G	G♯	A	A♯	B	C	C♯	D	D♯	E
12	11	10	9	8	7	6	5	4	3	2	1	0	1	2	3	4	5	6	7	8	9	10	11	12
	M3	P4		P5		M6		M7	OC		M2		M3	P4		P5		M6		M7	OC		M2	
m3			D5		m6		m7			m2		m3			D5		m6		m7			m2		m3
♯9		11	♯11			13				♭9	9	♯9		11	♯11			13				♭9	9	♯9

Key of E M3

E	F	F♯	G	G♯	A	A♯	B	C	C♯	D	D♯	E	F	F♯	G	G♯	A	A♯	B	C	C♯	D	D♯	E
12	11	10	9	8	7	6	5	4	3	2	1	0	1	2	3	4	5	6	7	8	9	10	11	12
M3	P4		P5		M6		M7	OC		M2		M3	P4		P5		M6		M7	OC		M2		M3
		D5		m6		m7			m2		m3			D5		m6		m7			m2		m3	
	11	♯11			13				♭9	9	♯9		11	♯11			13				♭9	9	♯9	

Key of E P4

E	F	F♯	G	G♯	A	A♯	B	C	C♯	D	D♯	E	F	F♯	G	G♯	A	A♯	B	C	C♯	D	D♯	E
12	**11**	**10**	**9**	**8**	**7**	**6**	**5**	**4**	**3**	**2**	**1**	**0**	**1**	**2**	**3**	**4**	**5**	**6**	**7**	**8**	**9**	**10**	**11**	**12**
P4		P5		M6		M7	OC		M2		M3	P4		P5		M6		M7	OC		M2		M3	P4
	D5		m6		m7			m2		m3			D5		m6		m7			m2		m3		
11	♯11			13				♭9	9	♯9		11	♯11			13				♭9	9	♯9		11

Key of E D5

E	F	F♯	G	G♯	A	A♯	B	C	C♯	D	D♯	E	F	F♯	G	G♯	A	A♯	B	C	C♯	D	D♯	E
12	**11**	**10**	**9**	**8**	**7**	**6**	**5**	**4**	**3**	**2**	**1**	**0**	**1**	**2**	**3**	**4**	**5**	**6**	**7**	**8**	**9**	**10**	**11**	**12**
	P5		M6		M7	OC		M2		M3	P4		P5		M6		M7	OC		M2		M3	P4	
D5		m6		m7			m2		m3			D5		m6		m7			m2		m3			D5
♯11			13				♭9	9	♯9		11	♯11			13				♭9	9	♯9		11	♯11

Key of E P5

E	F	F♯	G	G♯	A	A♯	B	C	C♯	D	D♯	E	F	F♯	G	G♯	A	A♯	B	C	C♯	D	D♯	E
12	**11**	**10**	**9**	**8**	**7**	**6**	**5**	**4**	**3**	**2**	**1**	**0**	**1**	**2**	**3**	**4**	**5**	**6**	**7**	**8**	**9**	**10**	**11**	**12**
P5		M6		M7	OC		M2		M3	P4		P5		M6		M7	OC		M2		M3	P4		P5
	m6		m7			m2		m3			D5		m6		m7			m2		m3			D5	
		13				♭9	9	♯9		11	♯11			13				♭9	9	♯9		11	♯11	

Key of E m6

E	F	F♯	G	G♯	A	A♯	B	C	C♯	D	D♯	E	F	F♯	G	G♯	A	A♯	B	C	C♯	D	D♯	E
12	**11**	**10**	**9**	**8**	**7**	**6**	**5**	**4**	**3**	**2**	**1**	**0**	**1**	**2**	**3**	**4**	**5**	**6**	**7**	**8**	**9**	**10**	**11**	**12**
	M6		M7	OC		M2		M3	P4		P5		M6		M7	OC		M2		M3	P4		P5	
m6		m7			m2		m3			D5		m6		m7			m2		m3			D5		m6
	13				♭9	9	♯9		11	♯11			13				♭9	9	♯9		11	♯11		

Key of E M6

E	F	F♯	G	G♯	A	A♯	B	C	C♯	D	D♯	E	F	F♯	G	G♯	A	A♯	B	C	C♯	D	D♯	E
12	**11**	**10**	**9**	**8**	**7**	**6**	**5**	**4**	**3**	**2**	**1**	**0**	**1**	**2**	**3**	**4**	**5**	**6**	**7**	**8**	**9**	**10**	**11**	**12**
M6		M7	OC		M2		M3	P4		P5		M6		M7	OC		M2		M3	P4		P5		M6
	m7			m2		m3			D5		m6		m7			m2		m3			D5		m6	
13				♭9	9	♯9		11	♯11			13				♭9	9	♯9		11	♯11			13

Key of E m7

E	F	F♯	G	G♯	A	A♯	B	C	C♯	D	D♯	E	F	F♯	G	G♯	A	A♯	B	C	C♯	D	D♯	E
12	**11**	**10**	**9**	**8**	**7**	**6**	**5**	**4**	**3**	**2**	**1**	**0**	**1**	**2**	**3**	**4**	**5**	**6**	**7**	**8**	**9**	**10**	**11**	**12**
	M7	OC		M2		M3	P4		P5		M6		M7	OC		M2		M3	P4		P5		M6	
m7			m2		m3			D5		m6		m7			m2		m3			D5		m6		m7
			♭9	9	♯9		11	♯11			13				♭9	9	♯9		11	♯11			13	

Key of E M7

E	F	F♯	G	G♯	A	A♯	B	C	C♯	D	D♯	E	F	F♯	G	G♯	A	A♯	B	C	C♯	D	D♯	E
12	**11**	**10**	**9**	**8**	**7**	**6**	**5**	**4**	**3**	**2**	**1**	**0**	**1**	**2**	**3**	**4**	**5**	**6**	**7**	**8**	**9**	**10**	**11**	**12**
M7	OC		M2		M3	P4		P5		M6		M7	OC		M2		M3	P4		P5		M6		M7
		m2		m3			D5		m6		m7			m2		m3			D5		m6		m7	
		♭9	9	♯9		11	♯11			13				♭9	9	♯9		11	♯11			13		

Key of F (OC)

F	F♯	G	G♯	A	A♯	B	C	C♯	D	D♯	E	F	F♯	G	G♯	A	A♯	B	C	C♯	D	D♯	E	F
12	**11**	**10**	**9**	**8**	**7**	**6**	**5**	**4**	**3**	**2**	**1**	**0**	**1**	**2**	**3**	**4**	**5**	**6**	**7**	**8**	**9**	**10**	**11**	**12**
OC		M2		M3	P4		P5		M6		M7	OC		M2		M3	P4		P5		M6		M7	OC
	m2		m3			D5		m6		m7			m2		m3			D5		m6		m7		
	♭9	9	♯9		11	♯11			13				♭9	9	♯9		11	♯11			13			

Key of F m2

F	F♯	G	G♯	A	A♯	B	C	C♯	D	D♯	E	F	F♯	G	G♯	A	A♯	B	C	C♯	D	D♯	E	F
12	**11**	**10**	**9**	**8**	**7**	**6**	**5**	**4**	**3**	**2**	**1**	**0**	**1**	**2**	**3**	**4**	**5**	**6**	**7**	**8**	**9**	**10**	**11**	**12**
	M2		M3	P4		P5		M6		M7	OC		M2		M3	P4		P5		M6		M7	OC	
m2		m3			D5		m6		m7			m2		m3			D5		m6		m7			m2
♭9	9	♯9		11	♯11			13				♭9	9	♯9		11	♯11			13				♭9

Key of F M2

F	F♯	G	G♯	A	A♯	B	C	C♯	D	D♯	E	F	F♯	G	G♯	A	A♯	B	C	C♯	D	D♯	E	F
12	**11**	**10**	**9**	**8**	**7**	**6**	**5**	**4**	**3**	**2**	**1**	**0**	**1**	**2**	**3**	**4**	**5**	**6**	**7**	**8**	**9**	**10**	**11**	**12**
M2		M3	P4		P5		M6		M7	OC		M2		M3	P4		P5		M6		M7	OC		M2
	m3			D5		m6		m7			m2		m3			D5		m6		m7			m2	
9	♯9		11	♯11			13				♭9	9	♯9		11	♯11			13				♭9	9

Key of F m3

F	F♯	G	G♯	A	A♯	B	C	C♯	D	D♯	E	F	F♯	G	G♯	A	A♯	B	C	C♯	D	D♯	E	F
12	11	10	9	8	7	6	5	4	3	2	1	0	1	2	3	4	5	6	7	8	9	10	11	12
	M3	P4		P5		M6		M7	OC		M2		M3	P4		P5		M6		M7	OC		M2	
m3			D5		m6		m7			m2		m3			D5		m6		m7			m2		m3
♯9		11	♯11			13				♭9	9	♯9		11	♯11			13				♭9	9	♯9

Key of F M3

F	F♯	G	G♯	A	A♯	B	C	C♯	D	D♯	E	F	F♯	G	G♯	A	A♯	B	C	C♯	D	D♯	E	F
12	11	10	9	8	7	6	5	4	3	2	1	0	1	2	3	4	5	6	7	8	9	10	11	12
M3	P4		P5		M6		M7	OC		M2		M3	P4		P5		M6		M7	OC		M2		M3
		D5		m6		m7			m2		m3			D5		m6		m7			m2		m3	
	11	♯11			13				♭9	9	♯9		11	♯11			13				♭9	9	♯9	

Key of F P4

F	F♯	G	G♯	A	A♯	B	C	C♯	D	D♯	E	F	F♯	G	G♯	A	A♯	B	C	C♯	D	D♯	E	F
12	11	10	9	8	7	6	5	4	3	2	1	0	1	2	3	4	5	6	7	8	9	10	11	12
P4		P5		M6		M7	OC		M2		M3	P4		P5		M6		M7	OC		M2		M3	P4
	D5		m6		m7			m2		m3			D5		m6		m7			m2		m3		
11	♯11			13				♭9	9	♯9		11	♯11			13				♭9	9	♯9		11

Key of F D5

F	F♯	G	G♯	A	A♯	B	C	C♯	D	D♯	E	F	F♯	G	G♯	A	A♯	B	C	C♯	D	D♯	E	F
12	11	10	9	8	7	6	5	4	3	2	1	0	1	2	3	4	5	6	7	8	9	10	11	12
	P5		M6		M7	OC		M2		M3	P4		P5		M6		M7	OC		M2		M3	P4	
D5		m6		m7			m2		m3			D5		m6		m7			m2		m3			D5
♯11			13				♭9	9	♯9		11	♯11			13				♭9	9	♯9		11	♯11

Key of F P5

F	F♯	G	G♯	A	A♯	B	C	C♯	D	D♯	E	F	F♯	G	G♯	A	A♯	B	C	C♯	D	D♯	E	F
12	11	10	9	8	7	6	5	4	3	2	1	0	1	2	3	4	5	6	7	8	9	10	11	12
P5		M6		M7	OC		M2		M3	P4		P5		M6		M7	OC		M2		M3	P4		P5
	m6		m7			m2		m3			D5		m6		m7			m2		m3			D5	
		13				♭9	9	♯9		11	♯11			13				♭9	9	♯9		11	♯11	

Key of F m6

F	F♯	G	G♯	A	A♯	B	C	C♯	D	D♯	E	F	F♯	G	G♯	A	A♯	B	C	C♯	D	D♯	E	F
12	**11**	**10**	**9**	**8**	**7**	**6**	**5**	**4**	**3**	**2**	**1**	**0**	**1**	**2**	**3**	**4**	**5**	**6**	**7**	**8**	**9**	**10**	**11**	**12**
	M6		M7	OC		M2		M3	P4		P5		M6		M7	OC		M2		M3	P4		P5	
m6		m7			m2		m3			D5		m6		m7			m2		m3			D5		m6
	13				♭9	9	♯9		11	♯11			13				♭9	9	♯9		11	♯11		

Key of F M6

F	F♯	G	G♯	A	A♯	B	C	C♯	D	D♯	E	F	F♯	G	G♯	A	A♯	B	C	C♯	D	D♯	E	F
12	**11**	**10**	**9**	**8**	**7**	**6**	**5**	**4**	**3**	**2**	**1**	**0**	**1**	**2**	**3**	**4**	**5**	**6**	**7**	**8**	**9**	**10**	**11**	**12**
M6		M7	OC		M2		M3	P4		P5		M6		M7	OC		M2		M3	P4		P5		M6
	m7			m2		m3			D5		m6		m7			m2		m3			D5		m6	
13				♭9	9	♯9		11	♯11			13				♭9	9	♯9		11	♯11			13

Key of F m7

F	F♯	G	G♯	A	A♯	B	C	C♯	D	D♯	E	F	F♯	G	G♯	A	A♯	B	C	C♯	D	D♯	E	F
12	**11**	**10**	**9**	**8**	**7**	**6**	**5**	**4**	**3**	**2**	**1**	**0**	**1**	**2**	**3**	**4**	**5**	**6**	**7**	**8**	**9**	**10**	**11**	**12**
	M7	OC		M2		M3	P4		P5		M6		M7	OC		M2		M3	P4		P5		M6	
m7			m2		m3			D5		m6		m7			m2		m3			D5		m6		m7
			♭9	9	♯9		11	♯11			13				♭9	9	♯9		11	♯11			13	

Key of F M7

F	F♯	G	G♯	A	A♯	B	C	C♯	D	D♯	E	F	F♯	G	G♯	A	A♯	B	C	C♯	D	D♯	E	F
12	**11**	**10**	**9**	**8**	**7**	**6**	**5**	**4**	**3**	**2**	**1**	**0**	**1**	**2**	**3**	**4**	**5**	**6**	**7**	**8**	**9**	**10**	**11**	**12**
M7	OC		M2		M3	P4		P5		M6		M7	OC		M2		M3	P4		P5		M6		M7
		m2		m3			D5		m6		m7			m2		m3			D5		m6		m7	
		♭9	9	♯9		11	♯11			13				♭9	9	♯9		11	♯11			13		

Key of F♯ (OC)

F♯	G	G♯	A	A♯	B	C	C♯	D	D♯	E	F	F♯	G	G♯	A	A♯	B	C	C♯	D	D♯	E	F	F♯
12	**11**	**10**	**9**	**8**	**7**	**6**	**5**	**4**	**3**	**2**	**1**	**0**	**1**	**2**	**3**	**4**	**5**	**6**	**7**	**8**	**9**	**10**	**11**	**12**
OC		M2		M3	P4		P5		M6		M7	OC		M2		M3	P4		P5		M6		M7	OC
	m2		m3			D5		m6		m7			m2		m3			D5		m6		m7		
	♭9	9	♯9		11	♯11			13				♭9	9	♯9		11	♯11			13			

Key of F♯ m2

F♯	G	G♯	A	A♯	B	C	C♯	D	D♯	E	F	F♯	G	G♯	A	A♯	B	C	C♯	D	D♯	E	F	F♯
12	**11**	**10**	**9**	**8**	**7**	**6**	**5**	**4**	**3**	**2**	**1**	**0**	**1**	**2**	**3**	**4**	**5**	**6**	**7**	**8**	**9**	**10**	**11**	**12**
	M2		M3	P4		P5		M6		M7	OC		M2		M3	P4		P5		M6		M7	OC	
m2		m3			D5		m6		m7			m2		m3			D5		m6		m7			m2
♭9	9	♯9		11	♯11			13				♭9	9	♯9		11	♯11			13				♭9

Key of F♯ M2

F♯	G	G♯	A	A♯	B	C	C♯	D	D♯	E	F	F♯	G	G♯	A	A♯	B	C	C♯	D	D♯	E	F	F♯
12	**11**	**10**	**9**	**8**	**7**	**6**	**5**	**4**	**3**	**2**	**1**	**0**	**1**	**2**	**3**	**4**	**5**	**6**	**7**	**8**	**9**	**10**	**11**	**12**
M2		M3	P4		P5		M6		M7	OC		M2		M3	P4		P5		M6		M7	OC		M2
	m3			D5		m6		m7			m2		m3			D5		m6		m7			m2	
9	♯9		11	♯11			13				♭9	9	♯9		11	♯11			13				♭9	9

Key of F♯ m3

F♯	G	G♯	A	A♯	B	C	C♯	D	D♯	E	F	F♯	G	G♯	A	A♯	B	C	C♯	D	D♯	E	F	F♯
12	**11**	**10**	**9**	**8**	**7**	**6**	**5**	**4**	**3**	**2**	**1**	**0**	**1**	**2**	**3**	**4**	**5**	**6**	**7**	**8**	**9**	**10**	**11**	**12**
	M3	P4		P5		M6		M7	OC		M2		M3	P4		P5		M6		M7	OC		M2	
m3			D5		m6		m7			m2		m3			D5		m6		m7			m2		m3
♯9		11	♯11			13				♭9	9	♯9		11	♯11			13				♭9	9	♯9

Key of F♯ M3

F♯	G	G♯	A	A♯	B	C	C♯	D	D♯	E	F	F♯	G	G♯	A	A♯	B	C	C♯	D	D♯	E	F	F♯
12	**11**	**10**	**9**	**8**	**7**	**6**	**5**	**4**	**3**	**2**	**1**	**0**	**1**	**2**	**3**	**4**	**5**	**6**	**7**	**8**	**9**	**10**	**11**	**12**
M3	P4		P5		M6		M7	OC		M2		M3	P4		P5		M6		M7	OC		M2		M3
		D5		m6		m7			m2		m3			D5		m6		m7			m2		m3	
	11	♯11			13				♭9	9	♯9		11	♯11			13				♭9	9	♯9	

Key of F♯ P4

F♯	G	G♯	A	A♯	B	C	C♯	D	D♯	E	F	F♯	G	G♯	A	A♯	B	C	C♯	D	D♯	E	F	F♯
12	**11**	**10**	**9**	**8**	**7**	**6**	**5**	**4**	**3**	**2**	**1**	**0**	**1**	**2**	**3**	**4**	**5**	**6**	**7**	**8**	**9**	**10**	**11**	**12**
P4		P5		M6		M7	OC		M2		M3	P4		P5		M6		M7	OC		M2		M3	P4
	D5		m6		m7			m2		m3			D5		m6		m7			m2		m3		
11	♯11			13				♭9	9	♯9		11	♯11			13				♭9	9	♯9		11

Key of F♯ D5

F♯	G	G♯	A	A♯	B	C	C♯	D	D♯	E	F	F♯	G	G♯	A	A♯	B	C	C♯	D	D♯	E	F	F♯
12	**11**	**10**	**9**	**8**	**7**	**6**	**5**	**4**	**3**	**2**	**1**	**0**	**1**	**2**	**3**	**4**	**5**	**6**	**7**	**8**	**9**	**10**	**11**	**12**
	P5		M6		M7	OC		M2		M3	P4		P5		M6		M7	OC		M2		M3	P4	
D5		m6		m7			m2		m3			D5		m6		m7			m2		m3			D5
♯11			13				♭9	9	♯9		11	♯11			13				♭9	9	♯9		11	♯11

Key of F♯ P5

F♯	G	G♯	A	A♯	B	C	C♯	D	D♯	E	F	F♯	G	G♯	A	A♯	B	C	C♯	D	D♯	E	F	F♯
12	**11**	**10**	**9**	**8**	**7**	**6**	**5**	**4**	**3**	**2**	**1**	**0**	**1**	**2**	**3**	**4**	**5**	**6**	**7**	**8**	**9**	**10**	**11**	**12**
P5		M6		M7	OC		M2		M3	P4		P5		M6		M7	OC		M2		M3	P4		P5
	m6		m7			m2		m3			D5		m6		m7			m2		m3			D5	
		13				♭9	9	♯9		11	♯11			13				♭9	9	♯9		11	♯11	

Key of F♯ m6

F♯	G	G♯	A	A♯	B	C	C♯	D	D♯	E	F	F♯	G	G♯	A	A♯	B	C	C♯	D	D♯	E	F	F♯
12	**11**	**10**	**9**	**8**	**7**	**6**	**5**	**4**	**3**	**2**	**1**	**0**	**1**	**2**	**3**	**4**	**5**	**6**	**7**	**8**	**9**	**10**	**11**	**12**
	M6		M7	OC		M2		M3	P4		P5		M6		M7	OC		M2		M3	P4		P5	
m6		m7			m2		m3			D5		m6		m7			m2		m3			D5		m6
	13				♭9	9	♯9		11	♯11			13				♭9	9	♯9		11	♯11		

Key of F♯ M6

F♯	G	G♯	A	A♯	B	C	C♯	D	D♯	E	F	F♯	G	G♯	A	A♯	B	C	C♯	D	D♯	E	F	F♯
12	**11**	**10**	**9**	**8**	**7**	**6**	**5**	**4**	**3**	**2**	**1**	**0**	**1**	**2**	**3**	**4**	**5**	**6**	**7**	**8**	**9**	**10**	**11**	**12**
M6		M7	OC		M2		M3	P4		P5		M6		M7	OC		M2		M3	P4		P5		M6
	m7			m2		m3			D5		m6		m7			m2		m3			D5		m6	
13				♭9	9	♯9		11	♯11			13				♭9	9	♯9		11	♯11			13

Key of F♯ m7

F♯	G	G♯	A	A♯	B	C	C♯	D	D♯	E	F	F♯	G	G♯	A	A♯	B	C	C♯	D	D♯	E	F	F♯
12	**11**	**10**	**9**	**8**	**7**	**6**	**5**	**4**	**3**	**2**	**1**	**0**	**1**	**2**	**3**	**4**	**5**	**6**	**7**	**8**	**9**	**10**	**11**	**12**
	M7	OC		M2		M3	P4		P5		M6		M7	OC		M2		M3	P4		P5		M6	
m7			m2		m3			D5		m6		m7			m2		m3			D5		m6		m7
			♭9	9	♯9		11	♯11			13				♭9	9	♯9		11	♯11			13	

Key of F♯ M7

F♯	G	G♯	A	A♯	B	C	C♯	D	D♯	E	F	F♯	G	G♯	A	A♯	B	C	C♯	D	D♯	E	F	F♯
12	11	10	9	8	7	6	5	4	3	2	1	0	1	2	3	4	5	6	7	8	9	10	11	12
M7	OC		M2		M3	P4		P5		M6		M7	OC		M2		M3	P4		P5		M6		M7
		m2		m3			D5		m6		m7			m2		m3			D5		m6		m7	
		♭9	9	♯9		11	♯11			13				♭9	9	♯9		11	♯11			13		

Key of G (OC)

G	G♯	A	A♯	B	C	C♯	D	D♯	E	F	F♯	G	G♯	A	A♯	B	C	C♯	D	D♯	E	F	F♯	G
12	11	10	9	8	7	6	5	4	3	2	1	0	1	2	3	4	5	6	7	8	9	10	11	12
OC		M2		M3	P4		P5		M6		M7	OC		M2		M3	P4		P5		M6		M7	OC
	m2		m3			D5		m6		m7			m2		m3			D5		m6		m7		
	♭9	9	♯9		11	♯11			13				♭9	9	♯9		11	♯11			13			

Key of G m2

G	G♯	A	A♯	B	C	C♯	D	D♯	E	F	F♯	G	G♯	A	A♯	B	C	C♯	D	D♯	E	F	F♯	G
12	11	10	9	8	7	6	5	4	3	2	1	0	1	2	3	4	5	6	7	8	9	10	11	12
	M2		M3	P4		P5		M6		M7	OC		M2		M3	P4		P5		M6		M7	OC	
m2		m3			D5		m6		m7			m2		m3			D5		m6		m7			m2
♭9	9	♯9		11	♯11			13				♭9	9	♯9		11	♯11			13				♭9

Key of G M2

G	G♯	A	A♯	B	C	C♯	D	D♯	E	F	F♯	G	G♯	A	A♯	B	C	C♯	D	D♯	E	F	F♯	G
12	11	10	9	8	7	6	5	4	3	2	1	0	1	2	3	4	5	6	7	8	9	10	11	12
M2		M3	P4		P5		M6		M7	OC		M2		M3	P4		P5		M6		M7	OC		M2
	m3			D5		m6		m7			m2		m3			D5		m6		m7			m2	
9	♯9		11	♯11			13				♭9	9	♯9		11	♯11			13				♭9	9

Key of G m3

G	G♯	A	A♯	B	C	C♯	D	D♯	E	F	F♯	G	G♯	A	A♯	B	C	C♯	D	D♯	E	F	F♯	G
12	11	10	9	8	7	6	5	4	3	2	1	0	1	2	3	4	5	6	7	8	9	10	11	12
	M3	P4		P5		M6		M7	OC		M2		M3	P4		P5		M6		M7	OC		M2	
m3			D5		m6		m7			m2		m3			D5		m6		m7			m2		m3
♯9		11	♯11			13				♭9	9	♯9		11	♯11			13				♭9	9	♯9

Key of G M3

G	G♯	A	A♯	B	C	C♯	D	D♯	E	F	F♯	G	G♯	A	A♯	B	C	C♯	D	D♯	E	F	F♯	G
12	11	10	9	8	7	6	5	4	3	2	1	0	1	2	3	4	5	6	7	8	9	10	11	12
M3	P4		P5		M6		M7	OC		M2		M3	P4		P5		M6		M7	OC		M2		M3
		D5		m6		m7			m2		m3			D5		m6		m7			m2		m3	
	11	♯11			13				♭9	9	♯9		11	♯11			13				♭9	9	♯9	

Key of G P4

G	G♯	A	A♯	B	C	C♯	D	D♯	E	F	F♯	G	G♯	A	A♯	B	C	C♯	D	D♯	E	F	F♯	G
12	11	10	9	8	7	6	5	4	3	2	1	0	1	2	3	4	5	6	7	8	9	10	11	12
P4		P5		M6		M7	OC		M2		M3	P4		P5		M6		M7	OC		M2		M3	P4
	D5		m6		m7			m2		m3			D5		m6		m7			m2		m3		
11	♯11			13				♭9	9	♯9		11	♯11			13				♭9	9	♯9		11

Key of G D5

G	G♯	A	A♯	B	C	C♯	D	D♯	E	F	F♯	G	G♯	A	A♯	B	C	C♯	D	D♯	E	F	F♯	G
12	11	10	9	8	7	6	5	4	3	2	1	0	1	2	3	4	5	6	7	8	9	10	11	12
	P5		M6		M7	OC		M2		M3	P4		P5		M6		M7	OC		M2		M3	P4	
D5		m6		m7			m2		m3			D5		m6		m7			m2		m3			D5
♯11			13				♭9	9	♯9		11	♯11			13				♭9	9	♯9		11	♯11

Key of G P5

G	G♯	A	A♯	B	C	C♯	D	D♯	E	F	F♯	G	G♯	A	A♯	B	C	C♯	D	D♯	E	F	F♯	G
12	11	10	9	8	7	6	5	4	3	2	1	0	1	2	3	4	5	6	7	8	9	10	11	12
P5		M6		M7	OC		M2		M3	P4		P5		M6		M7	OC		M2		M3	P4		P5
	m6		m7			m2		m3			D5		m6		m7			m2		m3			D5	
		13				♭9	9	♯9		11	♯11			13				♭9	9	♯9		11	♯11	

Key of G m6

G	G♯	A	A♯	B	C	C♯	D	D♯	E	F	F♯	G	G♯	A	A♯	B	C	C♯	D	D♯	E	F	F♯	G
12	11	10	9	8	7	6	5	4	3	2	1	0	1	2	3	4	5	6	7	8	9	10	11	12
	M6		M7	OC		M2		M3	P4		P5		M6		M7	OC		M2		M3	P4		P5	
m6		m7			m2		m3			D5		m6		m7			m2		m3			D5		m6
	13				♭9	9	♯9		11	♯11			13				♭9	9	♯9		11	♯11		

Key of G M6

G	G♯	A	A♯	B	C	C♯	D	D♯	E	F	F♯	G	G♯	A	A♯	B	C	C♯	D	D♯	E	F	F♯	G
12	**11**	**10**	**9**	**8**	**7**	**6**	**5**	**4**	**3**	**2**	**1**	**0**	**1**	**2**	**3**	**4**	**5**	**6**	**7**	**8**	**9**	**10**	**11**	**12**
M6		M7	OC		M2		M3	P4		P5		M6		M7	OC		M2		M3	P4		P5		M6
	m7			m2		m3			D5		m6		m7			m2		m3			D5		m6	
13				♭9	9	♯9		11	♯11			13				♭9	9	♯9		11	♯11			13

Key of G m7

G	G♯	A	A♯	B	C	C♯	D	D♯	E	F	F♯	G	G♯	A	A♯	B	C	C♯	D	D♯	E	F	F♯	G
12	**11**	**10**	**9**	**8**	**7**	**6**	**5**	**4**	**3**	**2**	**1**	**0**	**1**	**2**	**3**	**4**	**5**	**6**	**7**	**8**	**9**	**10**	**11**	**12**
	M7	OC		M2		M3	P4		P5		M6		M7	OC		M2		M3	P4		P5		M6	
m7			m2		m3			D5		m6		m7			m2		m3			D5		m6		m7
			♭9	9	♯9		11	♯11			13				♭9	9	♯9		11	♯11			13	

Key of G M7

G	G♯	A	A♯	B	C	C♯	D	D♯	E	F	F♯	G	G♯	A	A♯	B	C	C♯	D	D♯	E	F	F♯	G
12	**11**	**10**	**9**	**8**	**7**	**6**	**5**	**4**	**3**	**2**	**1**	**0**	**1**	**2**	**3**	**4**	**5**	**6**	**7**	**8**	**9**	**10**	**11**	**12**
M7	OC		M2		M3	P4		P5		M6		M7	OC		M2		M3	P4		P5		M6		M7
		m2		m3			D5		m6		m7			m2		m3			D5		m6		m7	
		♭9	9	♯9		11	♯11			13				♭9	9	♯9		11	♯11			13		

Key of G♯ (OC)

G♯	A	A♯	B	C	C♯	D	D♯	E	F	F♯	G	G♯	A	A♯	B	C	C♯	D	D♯	E	F	F♯	G	G♯
12	**11**	**10**	**9**	**8**	**7**	**6**	**5**	**4**	**3**	**2**	**1**	**0**	**1**	**2**	**3**	**4**	**5**	**6**	**7**	**8**	**9**	**10**	**11**	**12**
OC		M2		M3	P4		P5		M6		M7	OC		M2		M3	P4		P5		M6		M7	OC
	m2		m3			D5		m6		m7			m2		m3			D5		m6		m7		
	♭9	9	♯9		11	♯11			13				♭9	9	♯9		11	♯11			13			

Key of G♯ m2

G♯	A	A♯	B	C	C♯	D	D♯	E	F	F♯	G	G♯	A	A♯	B	C	C♯	D	D♯	E	F	F♯	G	G♯
12	**11**	**10**	**9**	**8**	**7**	**6**	**5**	**4**	**3**	**2**	**1**	**0**	**1**	**2**	**3**	**4**	**5**	**6**	**7**	**8**	**9**	**10**	**11**	**12**
	M2		M3	P4		P5		M6		M7	OC		M2		M3	P4		P5		M6		M7	OC	
m2		m3			D5		m6		m7			m2		m3			D5		m6		m7			m2
♭9	9	♯9		11	♯11		13					♭9	9	♯9		11	♯11			13				♭9

Key of G♯ M2

G♯	A	A♯	B	C	C♯	D	D♯	E	F	F♯	G	G♯	A	A♯	B	C	C♯	D	D♯	E	F	F♯	G	G♯
12	**11**	**10**	**9**	**8**	**7**	**6**	**5**	**4**	**3**	**2**	**1**	**0**	**1**	**2**	**3**	**4**	**5**	**6**	**7**	**8**	**9**	**10**	**11**	**12**
M2		M3	P4		P5		M6		M7	OC		M2		M3	P4		P5		M6		M7	OC		M2
	m3			D5		m6		m7			m2		m3			D5		m6		m7			m2	
9	♯9		11	♯11			13				♭9	9	♯9		11	♯11			13				♭9	9

Key of G♯ m3

G♯	A	A♯	B	C	C♯	D	D♯	E	F	F♯	G	G♯	A	A♯	B	C	C♯	D	D♯	E	F	F♯	G	G♯
12	**11**	**10**	**9**	**8**	**7**	**6**	**5**	**4**	**3**	**2**	**1**	**0**	**1**	**2**	**3**	**4**	**5**	**6**	**7**	**8**	**9**	**10**	**11**	**12**
	M3	P4		P5		M6		M7	OC		M2		M3	P4		P5		M6		M7	OC		M2	
m3			D5		m6		m7			m2		m3			D5		m6		m7			m2		m3
♯9		11	♯11			13				♭9	9	♯9		11	♯11			13				♭9	9	♯9

Key of G♯ M3

G♯	A	A♯	B	C	C♯	D	D♯	E	F	F♯	G	G♯	A	A♯	B	C	C♯	D	D♯	E	F	F♯	G	G♯
12	**11**	**10**	**9**	**8**	**7**	**6**	**5**	**4**	**3**	**2**	**1**	**0**	**1**	**2**	**3**	**4**	**5**	**6**	**7**	**8**	**9**	**10**	**11**	**12**
M3	P4		P5		M6		M7	OC		M2		M3	P4		P5		M6		M7	OC		M2		M3
		D5		m6		m7			m2		m3			D5		m6		m7			m2		m3	
	11	♯11			13				♭9	9	♯9		11	♯11			13				♭9	9	♯9	

Key of G♯ P4

G♯	A	A♯	B	C	C♯	D	D♯	E	F	F♯	G	G♯	A	A♯	B	C	C♯	D	D♯	E	F	F♯	G	G♯
12	**11**	**10**	**9**	**8**	**7**	**6**	**5**	**4**	**3**	**2**	**1**	**0**	**1**	**2**	**3**	**4**	**5**	**6**	**7**	**8**	**9**	**10**	**11**	**12**
P4		P5		M6		M7	OC		M2		M3	P4		P5		M6		M7	OC		M2		M3	P4
	D5		m6		m7			m2		m3			D5		m6		m7			m2		m3		
11	♯11			13				♭9	9	♯9		11	♯11			13				♭9	9	♯9		11

Key of G♯ D5

G♯	A	A♯	B	C	C♯	D	D♯	E	F	F♯	G	G♯	A	A♯	B	C	C♯	D	D♯	E	F	F♯	G	G♯
12	**11**	**10**	**9**	**8**	**7**	**6**	**5**	**4**	**3**	**2**	**1**	**0**	**1**	**2**	**3**	**4**	**5**	**6**	**7**	**8**	**9**	**10**	**11**	**12**
	P5		M6		M7	OC		M2		M3	P4		P5		M6		M7	OC		M2		M3	P4	
D5		m6		m7			m2		m3			D5		m6		m7			m2		m3			D5
♯11			13				♭9	9	♯9		11	♯11			13				♭9	9	♯9		11	♯11

Key of G♯ P5

G♯	A	A♯	B	C	C♯	D	D♯	E	F	F♯	G	G♯	A	A♯	B	C	C♯	D	D♯	E	F	F♯	G	G♯
12	11	10	9	8	7	6	5	4	3	2	1	0	1	2	3	4	5	6	7	8	9	10	11	12
P5		M6		M7	OC		M2		M3	P4		P5		M6		M7	OC		M2		M3	P4		P5
	m6		m7			m2		m3			D5		m6		m7			m2		m3			D5	
		13				♭9	9	♯9		11	♯11			13				♭9	9	♯9		11	♯11	

Key of G♯ m6

G♯	A	A♯	B	C	C♯	D	D♯	E	F	F♯	G	G♯	A	A♯	B	C	C♯	D	D♯	E	F	F♯	G	G♯
12	11	10	9	8	7	6	5	4	3	2	1	0	1	2	3	4	5	6	7	8	9	10	11	12
	M6		M7	OC		M2		M3	P4		P5		M6		M7	OC		M2		M3	P4		P5	
m6		m7			m2		m3			D5		m6		m7			m2		m3			D5		m6
	13				♭9	9	♯9		11	♯11			13				♭9	9	♯9		11	♯11		

Key of G♯ M6

G♯	A	A♯	B	C	C♯	D	D♯	E	F	F♯	G	G♯	A	A♯	B	C	C♯	D	D♯	E	F	F♯	G	G♯
12	11	10	9	8	7	6	5	4	3	2	1	0	1	2	3	4	5	6	7	8	9	10	11	12
M6		M7	OC		M2		M3	P4		P5		M6		M7	OC		M2		M3	P4		P5		M6
	m7			m2		m3			D5		m6		m7			m2		m3			D5		m6	
13				♭9	9	♯9		11	♯11			13				♭9	9	♯9		11	♯11			13

Key of G♯ m7

G♯	A	A♯	B	C	C♯	D	D♯	E	F	F♯	G	G♯	A	A♯	B	C	C♯	D	D♯	E	F	F♯	G	G♯
12	11	10	9	8	7	6	5	4	3	2	1	0	1	2	3	4	5	6	7	8	9	10	11	12
	M7	OC		M2		M3	P4		P5		M6		M7	OC		M2		M3	P4		P5		M6	
m7			m2		m3			D5		m6		m7			m2		m3			D5		m6		m7
			♭9	9	♯9		11	♯11			13				♭9	9	♯9		11	♯11			13	

Key of G♯ M7

G♯	A	A♯	B	C	C♯	D	D♯	E	F	F♯	G	G♯	A	A♯	B	C	C♯	D	D♯	E	F	F♯	G	G♯
12	11	10	9	8	7	6	5	4	3	2	1	0	1	2	3	4	5	6	7	8	9	10	11	12
M7	OC		M2		M3	P4		P5		M6		M7	OC		M2		M3	P4		P5		M6		M7
		m2		m3			D5		m6		m7			m2		m3			D5		m6		m7	
		♭9	9	♯9		11	♯11			13				♭9	9	♯9		11	♯11			13		

The Equalizer - A Musical Method and Chord Progressions

Symmetrical Chord Progressions - progressions that are built on the principle that chords are selected from the balance-beam chart based on the fact that they are the same distance above and below the key note. for example, selecting the note seven frets below (perfect fourth) the key note and seven frets above (perfect fifth) the key note, on the guitar. This is a perfect symmetrical progression.

Diverse Chord Progressions - progressions that are selected from the balance-beam chart, based on the fact that they agree in number on both sides of the balance-beam. However, they are not symmetrical.

Examples

The first example is a symmetrical progression taken from the C M3 Interval Balance-Beam Chart. Note how they are the same distance, the seventh (7th) position, from the root note. As shown in example 1.

Example 1

Key of C M3

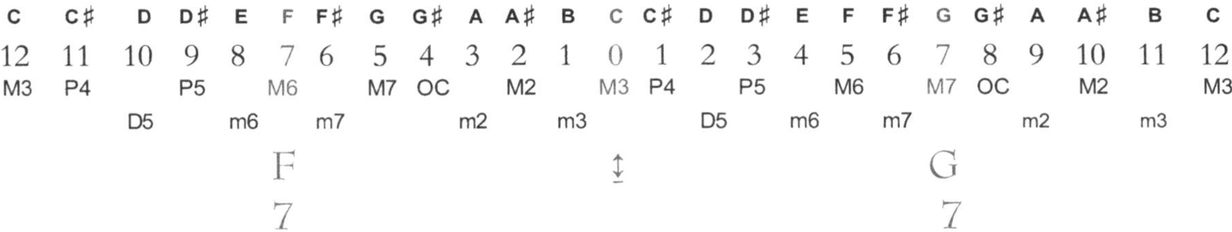

C	C♯	D	D♯	E	F	F♯	G	G♯	A	A♯	B	C	C♯	D	D♯	E	F	F♯	G	G♯	A	A♯	B	C
12	11	10	9	8	7	6	5	4	3	2	1	0	1	2	3	4	5	6	7	8	9	10	11	12
M3	P4		P5		M6		M7	OC		M2		M3	P4		P5		M6		M7	OC		M2		M3
		D5		m6		m7			m2		m3			D5		m6		m7			m2		m3	
					F							↕							G					
					7														7					

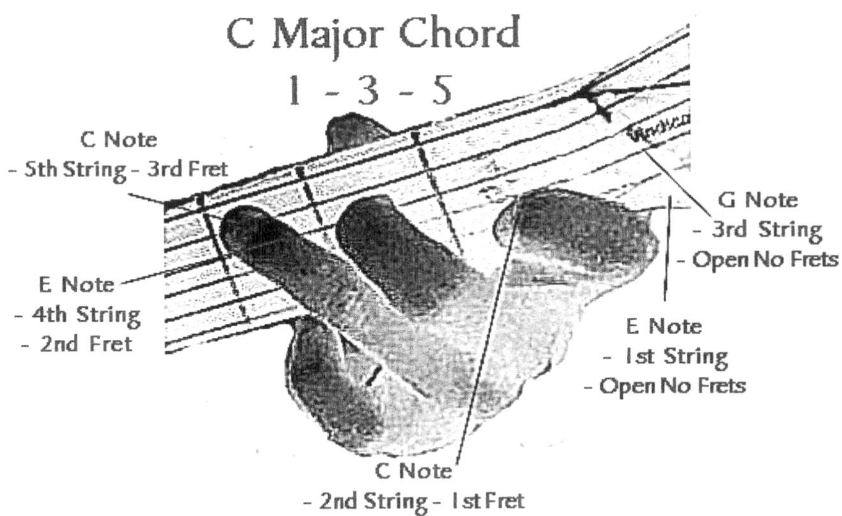

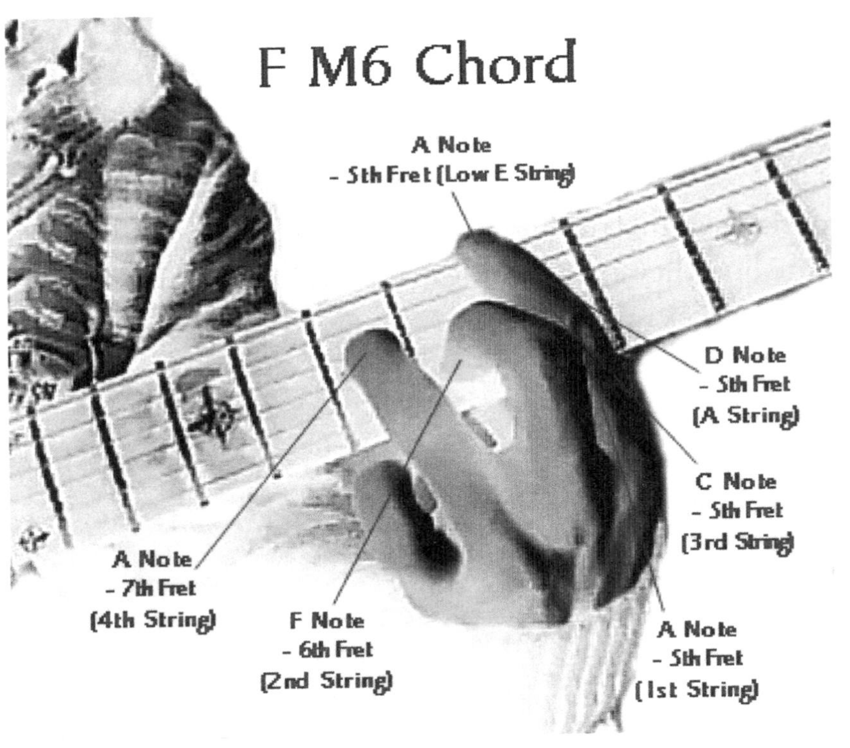
F M6 Chord
A Note
- 5th Fret (Low E String)
D Note
- 5th Fret
(A String)
C Note
- 5th Fret
(3rd String)
A Note
- 7th Fret
(4th String)
F Note
- 6th Fret
(2nd String)
A Note
- 5th Fret
(1st String)

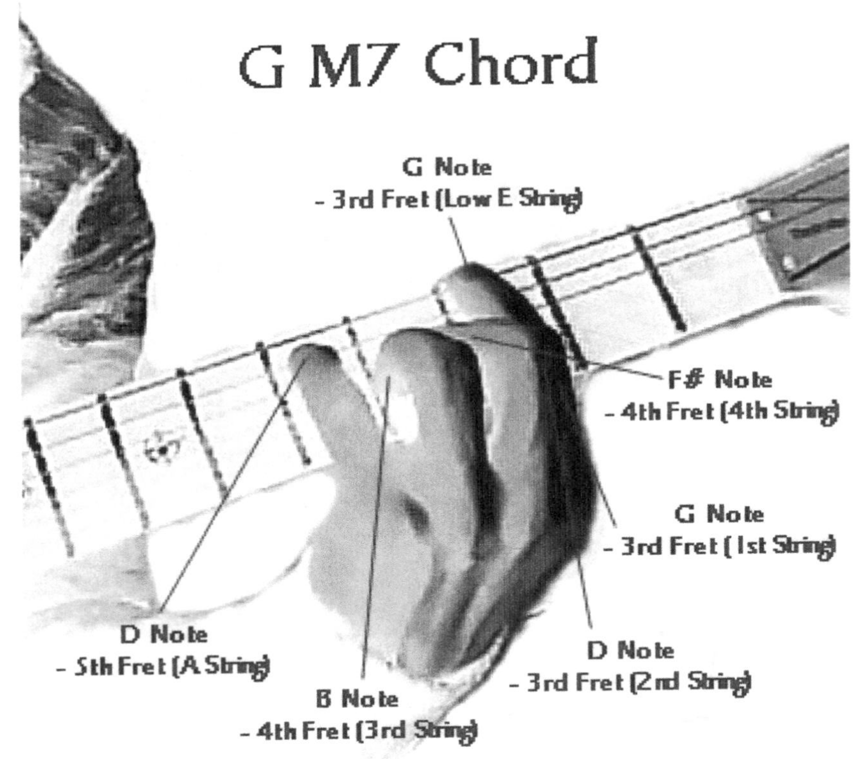
G M7 Chord
G Note
- 3rd Fret (Low E String)
F# Note
- 4th Fret (4th String)
G Note
- 3rd Fret (1st String)
D Note
- 5th Fret (A String)
D Note
- 3rd Fret (2nd String)
B Note
- 4th Fret (3rd String)

TAB
C Mjor Progression

```
       C Major      F M6      C Major       G M7
---------0-0---------5-5--------0-0----------3-3---
---------1-1-6-6-6-6------------1-1----------3-3---
---------0-0---------5-5--------0-0----------4-4---
---------2-2---------7-7--------2-2----------4-4---
-3-3-3-3-------------5-5-3-3-3-3-------------5-5---
---------3-3---------5-5--------3-3-3-3-3-3--------
```

The second example is a diverse progression taken from the Key of A m3 Balance-Beam Chart. On the right side of the Balance-Beam Chart you have the F M7 at the eithth (8) position. To balance the beam I used the F# Octave (OC) represented by three (3) and the E m7 and represented by five (5) on the left side of the beam to balance it. As shown in example 2.

Example 2

Key of A m3

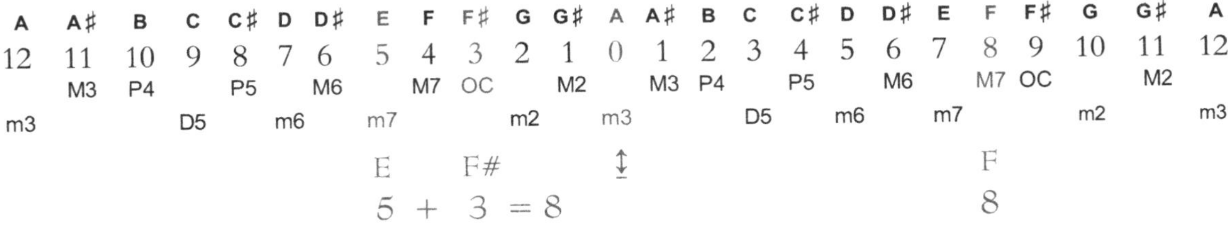

A Minor Chord

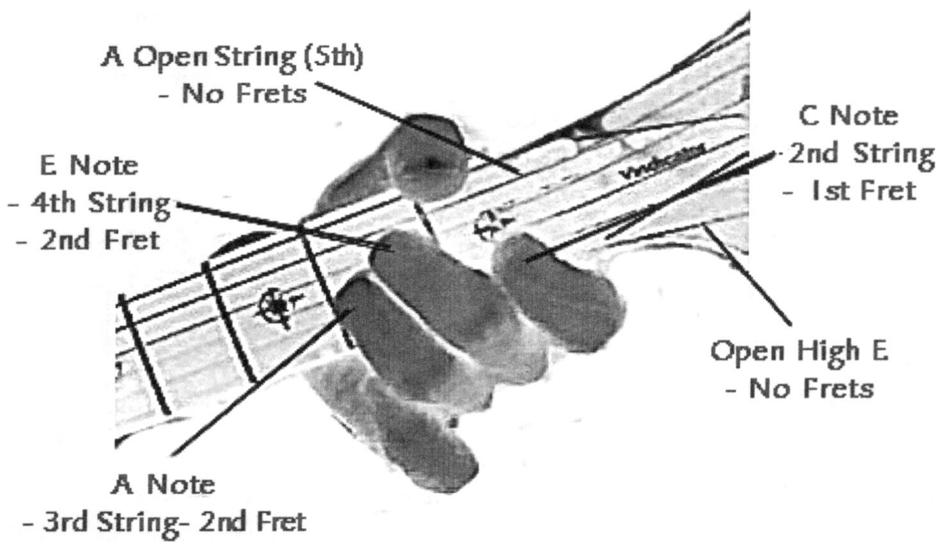

F M7 Chord

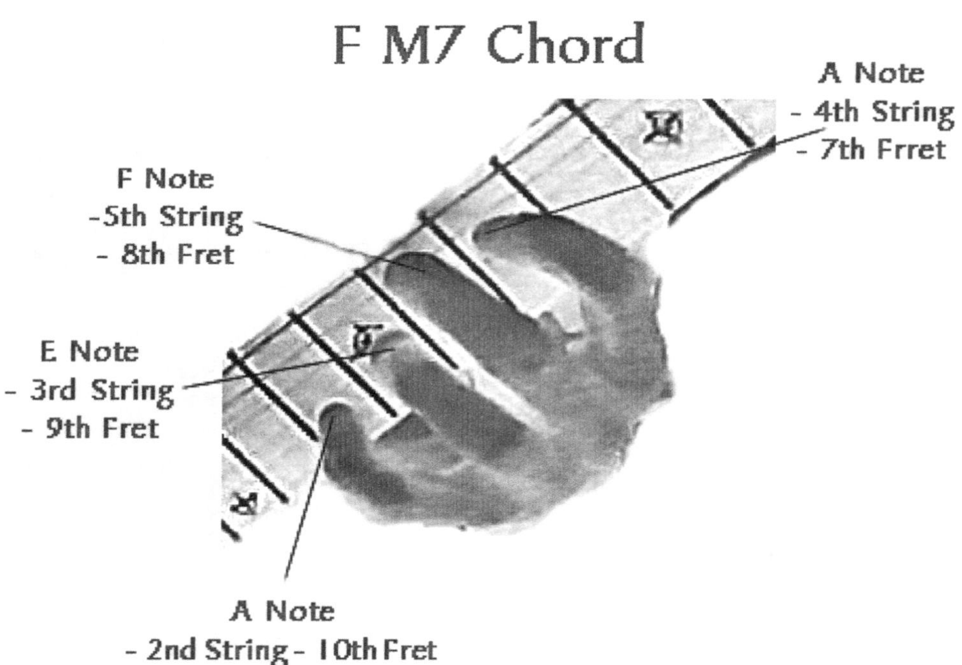

F# Octave Interval

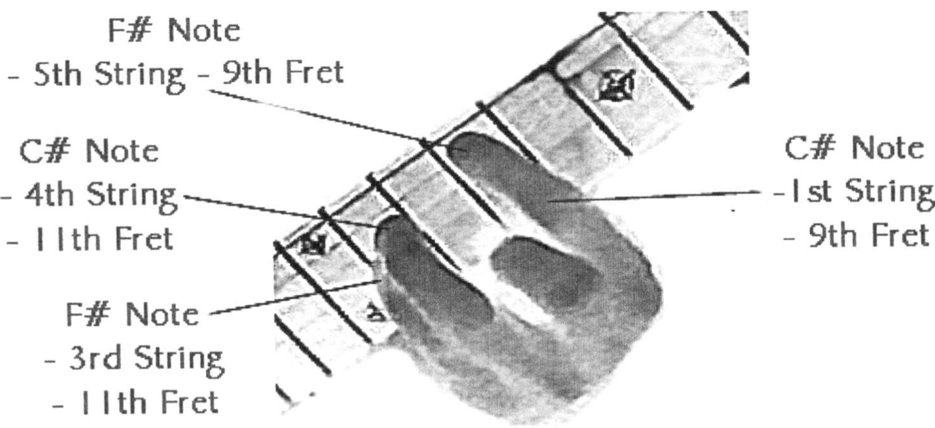

Em7 Chord

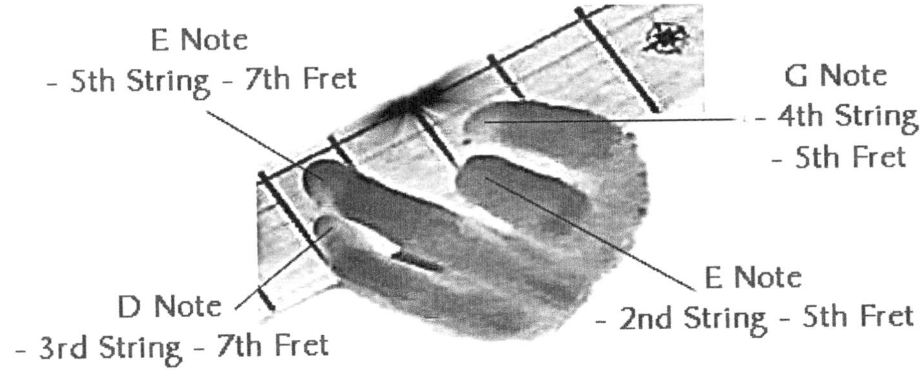

TAB
A Minor Chord Progression

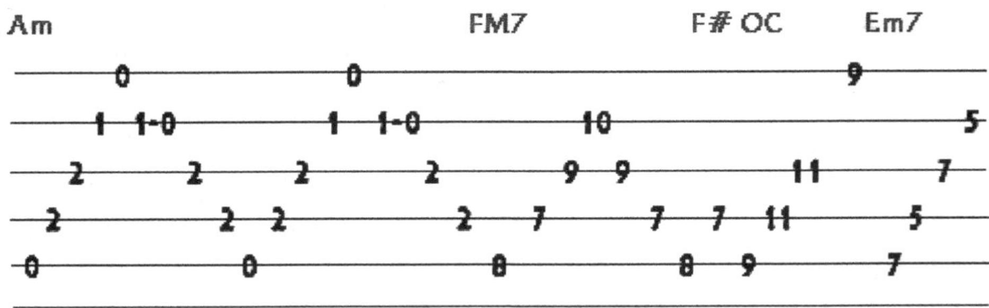

The third example is also a diverse progression taken from the Key of E M3 Balance-Beam Chart. I started with A M6 on the left side of the balance-beam, and is represented by seven (7). To balance it on the right side of the beam, I selected G# m6 represented by four (4) and the G P5 represented by three (3) to equal seven and balance the beam. As shown in example 3.

Example 3

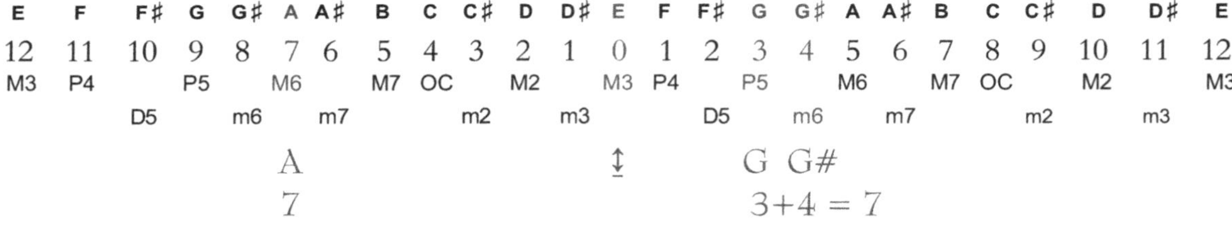

E M3 Interval

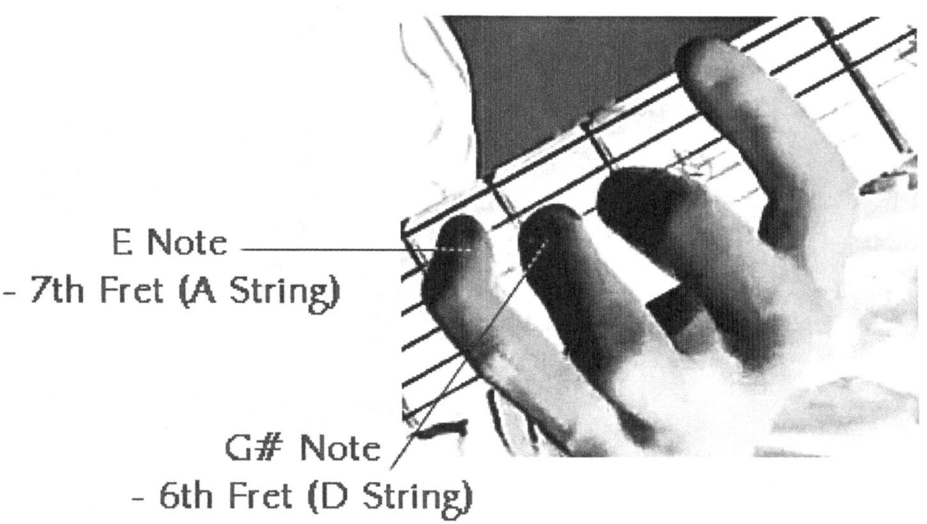

A M6 Interval

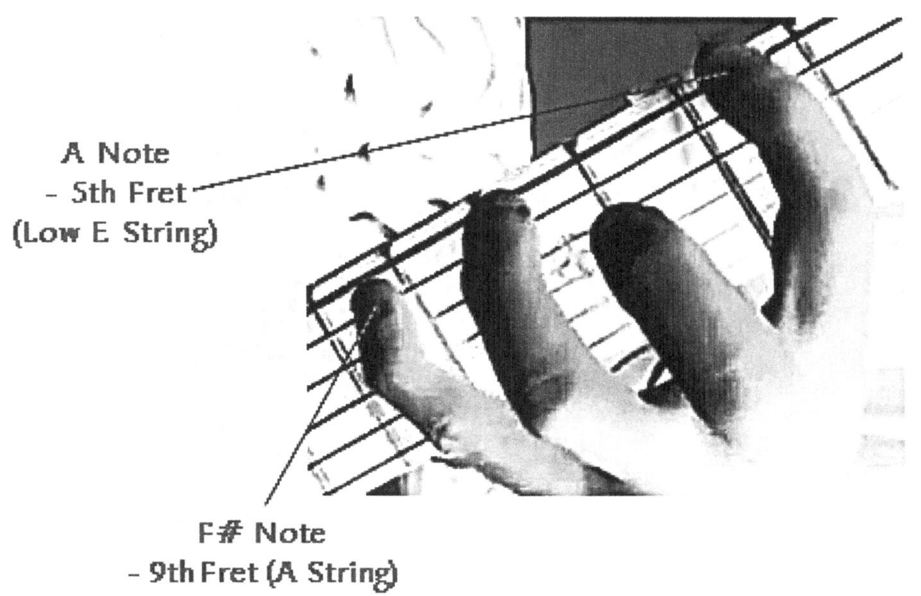

G# m6 Interval

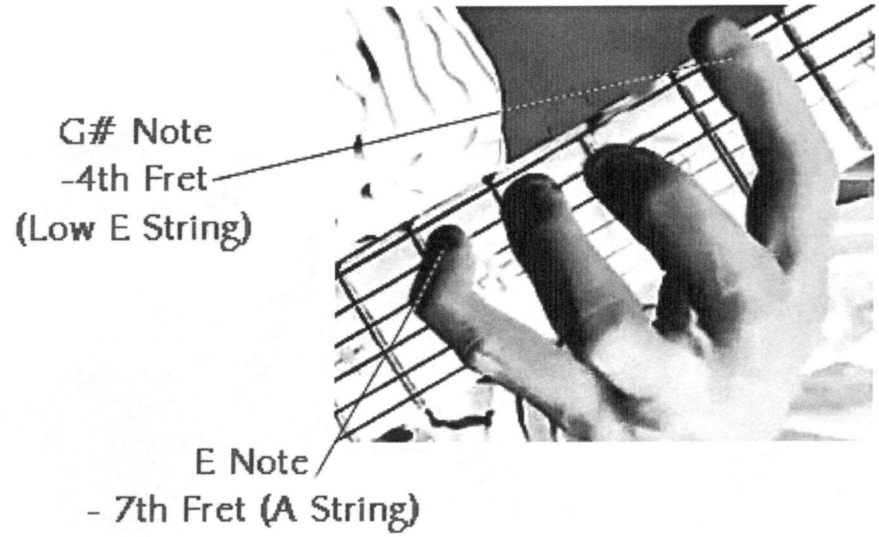

G P5 Interval

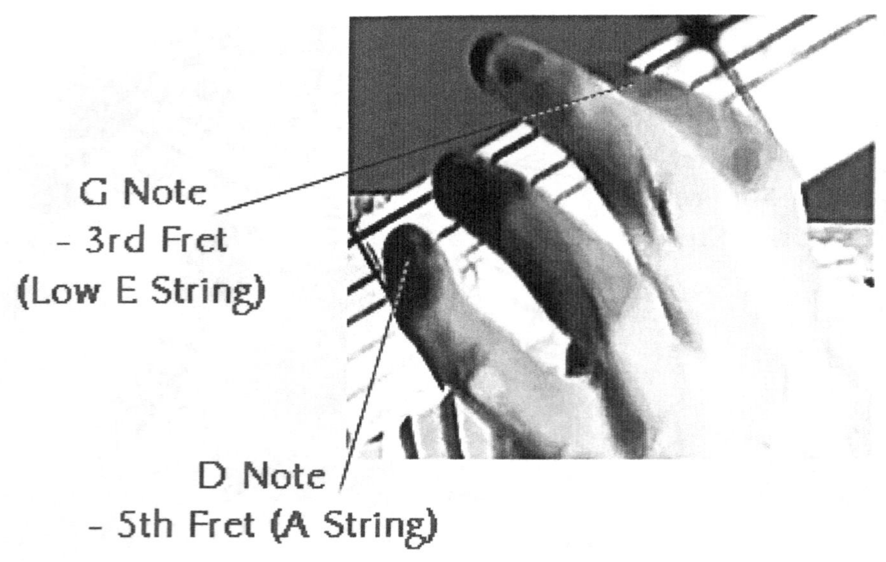

TAB
E M3 Progression

```
EM3             AM6                  G#m6  GP5
-------------------------------------------------
-------------------------------------------------
-------------------------------------------------
-------6-----------------------6-----------------
----7-----7-----9-----9-----7-----7--7--------5--
-0-----------0-----5-----0-----------------4--3---
```

About the Author

Craig Blake is an avid inventor, innovator, musician, fly-angler and writer. He resides in Happy Valley-Goose Bay, NL, Canada, with his wife Emma and their five children: Jako, Sheldon, Henrietta, Levi and Renee (Angel). Craig realized at an early age that he wanted to pursue a career in the world of business, and with business - communication is key.

Craig spends the cold Labrador winters studying, practicing and teaching music, and he spends his summers pursuing his other passion - fly fishing. Craig has been a professional fly-fishing guide for fifteen years in Labrador until his retirement. He has guided for Atlantic salmon and Eastern Brook trout. The notable places that he has guided include: Igloo Lake Lodge, Flower's River Lodge, Eagle River, Eagle Lake and Awesome Lake Lodge.

With Craig, every interest becomes a passion, and every passion becomes a dedicated study. It was through this dedicated study that he devised his own philosophy: - Realizing the potential of your instrument, is the instrument to realizing your potential. And this philosophy can be applied to any field of study. During his twenty four years of studying music Craig was always driven by one question: Why do the chord and note selections sound perfectly balanced? It was this nagging question that challenged him to create a system that would virtually eliminate all guess work and ultimately benefit the composer. The end result was The Equalizer - A Musical Method, a system of musical formulae that are based on notes, numbers and a balance beam.

The Equalizer
- A Musical Method

The Equalizer - A Musical Method is a natural and gravitational approach to song-writing by means of numbers and a balance-beam. Simply, create chord progressions with the balance-beam charts, then apply the compatible scales/scale-sets.

The Equalizer - A Musical Method can be incorporated by novice, intermediate, and advanced musicians, and it can also be applied to any genre of music such as rock, blues, jazz, country etc., by incorporating the balance beam - it opened up a-whole-new-world of possibilities. My mission: Strive to design a system for music-writing that would ultimately assist the composer during the development process.

Lightning Source UK Ltd.
Milton Keynes UK
UKOW07f1218310516

275322UK00001B/19/P